BRITAIN IN OLD PHOTOGRAPHS

MIDDLESEX

COUNTY CRICKET CLUB

WILLIAM A. POWELL

SUTTON PUBLISHING·LIMITED

Sutton Publishing Limited
Phoenix Mill · Thrupp · Stroud
Gloucestershire · GL5 2BU

First published 1999

Title page photograph: Middlesex double
champions, 1980.

British Library Cataloguing in Publication Data
A catalogue record for this book is available from the
British Library.

ISBN 0-7509-2138-2

Typeset in 10/11 Bembo.
Typesetting and origination by
Sutton Publishing Limited.
Printed in Great Britain by
Ebenezer Baylis, Worcester.

> *This book is dedicated to my dear friends Vic Lewis and Eddie Solomon,*
> *two of Middlesex's greatest supporters.*

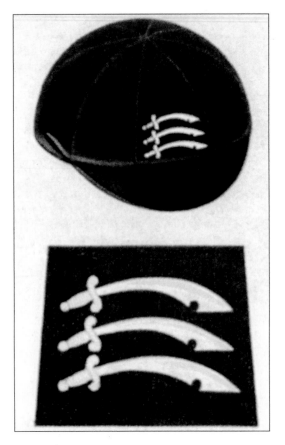

The famous three seaxes badge of the
Middlesex County Cricket Club, founded
in 1864 and based at Lord's Cricket Ground
in London NW8.

ACKNOWLEDGEMENTS

I would like to thank in particular the Middlesex County Cricket Club who kindly loaned me a wealth of photographic material for inclusion in the book from their archive photograph collection. Others are from my own postcard collection. I would also like to thank the following, who have assisted in a variety of ways in the preparation of this book:

Alex Bannister, Simon Fletcher, Annabel Fearnley, Mike Brearley OBE, John Warr, Brian A.C. Croudy, Vic Lewis, the late Ronald Harries, Eric Russell, Chris Lowe, Donald Carr OBE, Eddie Solomon, Peter W.G. Powell, John R. Lodge, Vinny Codrington, Eric Howes, Daphne Short, Giles Lyon, Joe Hardstaff, the late Ivan Alter, the late Bob Jones, the late Derek Lodge, Josh Fitch, Martin Wood, Sohail Malik, Andy West and Rupert Vitoria.

I acknowledge the sources of the illustrations which are many and include the Middlesex County Cricket Club archives including those of Adrian Murrell, Alan Cozzi, Barratt's, Benham, Bill Smith, Bob Thomas, British Telecom, Central Press, Creative Stills, Dennis Dobson, Derbyshire CCC, Edgar Asher, *Evening Standard*, Marylebone Cricket Club, Michael Stephens, *Middlesex County Press*, Patrick Eagar, Paul Lewis, Peter Phillips, Press Agency, Press Association, Sport & General, Stamp Publicity (Worthing), Steve Lindsell, Surrey CCC, Tom Morris, Universal, Vic Lewis, Western Australian Cricket Association and Wilkes & Son. County Print Services, Walker's Studios, the Harries family collection, the Vic Lewis collection and my own collection of picture postcards. Apologies are offered to anyone whose photographs have inadvertently been used without acknowledgement.

The 'Middlesex Twins': Bill Edrich and Denis Compton walk to the wicket at Lord's in 1947.

BIBLIOGRAPHY

C.W. Alcock, *Famous Cricketers and Cricket Grounds*, Hudson & Kearns, 1895

F.S. Ashley-Cooper, *Middlesex County Cricket Club 1900–1920*, Heinemann, 1921

Philip Bailey, Philip Thorn and Peter Wynne-Thomas *Who's Who of Cricketers*, Hamlyn, 1993

R.G. Barlow, *Forty Seasons of First-Class Cricket*, John Heywood, 1909

W.A. Bettsworth, *The Walkers of Southgate*, Methuen & Co., 1900

Percy Cross Standing, *Cricket of Today and Yesterday*, Vols I and II, Blackwood

William Dewar, *The Cricket Annual 1892*, Frank Fawcett, 1892

W.J. Ford, *Middlesex County Cricket Club 1864–1899*, Longman, Green & Co, 1900

Bill Frindall, *England Test Cricketers*, Collins Willow, 1989

N. Haig, *Middlesex County Cricket Club 1921–1947*, for the Club, 1949

Dean Hayes, *Famous Cricketers of Middlesex*, Spellmount, 1992

William A. Powell, *Cricket Grounds of Middlesex*, Association of Cricket Statisticians, 1990

William A. Powell, *Cricket Grounds Then and Now*, Ian Allan, 1994

William A. Powell, *The Wisden Guide to Cricket Grounds*, Stanley Paul, 1992

Terence Prittie, *Mainly Middlesex*, Hutchinson, 1946

Terence Prittie, *Middlesex,* County Cricket series, Convoy, 1951

Anton Rippon, *The Story of Middlesex County Cricket Club*, Moorland, 1982

E.M. Wellings, *A History of Middlesex*, Arthur Barker, 1972

Peter Wynne-Thomas, *Middlesex Cricketers 1864–1976*, Association of Cricket Statisticians, 1976

Cricket Weekly Record 1882 to 1913

The Cricketer International Magazine 1921 to 1998

James Lillywhite's Annuals 1882 to 1900

Middlesex County Cricket Club Review 1980/81 to 1997/98

Playfair Cricket Annuals 1948 to 1998

World of Cricket 1914

CONTENTS

FOREWORD

It is a very brave effort to attempt to capture the history, tradition and wide variety of people who have made up the rich tapestry of Middlesex County Cricket Club since its foundation in 1863. It is no coincidence that the first ground that Middlesex played on was owned by an innkeeper, starting a taste for conviviality which survives to this day. But the most important moment, rightly commemorated in this book, is the year 1877 when Middlesex started their long and distinguished association with Lord's Cricket Ground. In many ways, having Lord's as a home ground has been a double-edged sword for the club. It has, of course, been a great source of inspiration down the years for the many great players who have graced the hallowed turf playing for Middlesex County Cricket Club. Equally all the sides that come to Lord's are keen to give a good account of themselves at the headquarters of cricket. This has meant that games have been much harder to win over the years when the visitors are pumped up to give their utmost.

It has also made quite certain that the quality of cricket has been high with a premium on attractive play and the desire to get a result. Before the amateur became an extinct species, many great amateurs were attracted to play at Lord's because it was the height of their ambition. Indeed quite a number were also members of the MCC, which in a sense meant they were playing on their own home ground. Oxford and Cambridge provided many of these players and certainly in my time they always had a good relationship with the professionals on the staff. The days of professionals and amateurs using separate gates finished after the Second World War. Before the war, there was the famous occasion when ten amateurs took the field down the pavilion steps and 'Patsy' Hendren entered from the side as the only professional playing. But great professionals like the Hearnes, Hendren and Compton have been the backbone of the great playing tradition of the county club.

Although the MCC own and control Lord's it is interesting that four stands around the ground are dedicated to Middlesex cricketers: the Warner, Allen, Compton and Edrich Stands. This speaks volumes for the influence of Middlesex on the growth and development of Lord's, but Middlesex cricket is not confined to St John's Wood. Although it does not have the same spread of grounds that some counties have at their disposal, it has attempted to introduce the game to schools and clubs. As a geographical entity Middlesex has been incorporated into Greater London but this has not prevented a strong sense of loyalty to the three seaxes which make up the club's logo.

In the brave new world of two-division cricket which has been thrust upon us, I hope that the result of one year's performance will not mean second division cricket for a club that has contributed so much to the history and welfare of our great game.

John Warr

J.J. Warr
Holyport
Berkshire
January 1999

INTRODUCTION

A provisional committee circulated a letter to newspapers in 1863 which began with a challenge: 'Middlesex being the only cricketing county in England that has no county club . . . .' Its birth, a year later, coincided with the acceptance of over-arm bowling, and the first edition of John Wisden's *Cricketers' Almanack*.

The Walker brothers of Southgate, all seven of them, were prime movers in the launch and long continued to be influential on and off the field. When the championship was won in 1920, Sir Pelham Warner's last season, the president was R.D. Walker, who had been a member of the 1866 champions.

Several different grounds were used before Middlesex accepted an invitation by the MCC in 1877 to play at Lord's. Middlesex have been identified with Lord's ever since, and it has proved, a century later, to be no disadvantage to take part in knockout finals on their home ground. In eight finals they have won either the Gillette Cup or the NatWest Trophy in four out of six attempts, and the Benson & Hedges Cup twice with one defeat.

Middlesex's early reputation was identified with the dashing amateur batsman. The Fords, Studds and Lytteltons set a fashion of family links, which continued with the Manns, the Comptons and the Robins, father and son. The Hearne cousins from Buckinghamshire gave years of brilliant professional service. In one of his twelve Tests in 1899 at Headingley, John Thomas performed the famous hat trick, dismissing Clem Hill, Jack Gregory and Monty Noble, and John William (Young Jack) bowled his googlies like an angel. He formed with Elias 'Patsy' Hendren one of the most illustrious batting partnerships in county cricket. He scored 96 first-class centuries, took 1,839 wickets, and played in twenty-four Tests.

Among the captains to score in the grand manner was A.E. Stoddart, who led England in two of his four tours of Australia. His approach was summed up in a single word when Aussie propaganda tried to persuade him Monty Noble's flight was a problem for England. 'Rats', he snorted.

A wealth of talent was available up to 1914 including such names as Warner, Bosanquet, the inventor of the googly which he called the 'twist-twosti', A.J. Webbe, player, captain, honorary secretary and president over sixty-one years, Sir T.C. O'Brien, and the two Australian professionals, Albert Trott and Frank Tarrant. Gregor MacGregor was regarded as the finest wicket-keeper of his, or perhaps any, period.

Trott qualified after being omitted from his brother Harry's party to England in 1896, despite outstanding form against Stoddart's side in 1894-95. In his second and third seasons he took over 200 wickets and made 1,000 runs, and in 1899 straight drove the Lord's pavilion, a feat never accomplished before or since. In the end it did him no good as he often lost his wicket trying to repeat the shot.

His benefit in 1907 was ruined on the second day when he took four wickets with successive deliveries, and polished off the Somerset innings with a second hat trick. 'I bowled myself into the workhouse', he lamented. Brilliant though he was, there was a feeling that he could have been even better and his skipper MacGregor told him: 'If you had a head instead of a turnip, Alberto, you'd be the best bowler in the world.'

Tarrant, slow to medium left arm, averaged 100 wickets and 1,200 runs over a decade, and his ally J.W. Hearne provided Warner with a fine attack and runs. They did not reappear together after the First World War when Warner enriched his long career for club and country with Middlesex's third county championship. Warner was carried off the field in the last exciting match with neighbours and arch rivals Surrey.

Warner's life was given to cricket and his beloved Lord's, and only Sir George Allen can match the length, fidelity and variation of his stewardship. Gentlemen versus Players, a fixture long before Test matches were thought of, was the love of his sporting life, because it represented the fabric of first-class cricket in England. 'I pray and believe it will never die', wrote Warner. Fate decreed that he should die in 1963, the year after the decision was taken to do away with the distinction between amateur and professional, which meant a traditional fixture, started in 1806, was no longer played.

F.T. Mann succeeded Warner in 1921 and led the championship race from starter's pistol to tape, but, despite being able to call on the high talents of amateurs Allen, Stevens, Robins, Peebles, Haig, Enthoven, Killick and Owen-Smith, Middlesex had to wait until the Compton-Edrich run orgy of 1947 to taste championship victory again. The inability of the leading amateurs to play regularly, plus their absence on Test call, possibly cost Middlesex the honours, finishing third in 1935, and runners-up in the four years up to 1939, a position retained in the first season after the Second World War.

Hendren, with 170 centuries and 57,611 runs, and a splendid record in fifty-one Tests, was not merely a superb batsman and entertainer, but a personality who left a trail of warmth wherever he performed. Middlesex were singularly blessed when Compton and Edrich took over the mantle of Hendren and Hearne.

Denis Compton, also an Arsenal footballer, winner of FA Cup winners' medals and a wartime international, was the most glamorous sportsman of his day. He batted as if it was fun and not a grim technical exercise, and few bowlers succeeded in shackling his genius. Mere figures seem intruders within the radius of his unique skills, which had no affinity with the coaching manuals. But for a football injury he would have improved on his record of 123 first-class centuries; of these 17 were for England, and a record 18, with 3,816 runs, came in the fabulous summer of 1947 when the visiting South Africans also felt the whiplash of his remarkable form. 'Far from feeling tired I wished it could have gone on forever with the season never ending', Compton confessed. He served a demanding captain in Robins who asked for quick runs to leave time to bowl out his opponents twice. The first four in the Middlesex order – the thoroughbred Robertson, Brown,

Mr John Walker, 1847.

Edrich and Compton – responded with consistent brilliance. Centuries flowed from their bats, and remarkably Compton and Edrich augmented the bowling, which included the high-class spin of Sims and Young. Middlesex have rarely had a more eventful season.

One of Middlesex's finest spinners, Fred Titmus, collected 2,830 wickets with his off spin, and was a leading all-rounder in fifty-three Tests. Fast bowlers Alan Moss, John Warr, John Price, Wayne Daniel and Norman Cowans made a considerable impact, as did the spinners, John Emburey and Phil Edmonds. Peter Parfitt was invariably in the runs for both club and country, and John Murray with 1,527 victims, Leslie Compton and Paul Downton stand high in wicket-keeping ratings.

Mike Brearley, a man of scholarship and understanding, was a captain of rare talent. As a batsman he was perhaps half a class

Mr A.J. Webbe and Mr I.D. Walker.

short of Test match requirements, but he made useful scores, caught superbly at slip and was worth his weight in gold as an outstanding leader in the top drawer with Richie Benaud and Ray Illingworth.

Mike Gatting travelled the same road without the benefit of Brearley's apprenticeship of captaincy at Cambridge. He, too, returned from Australia a winning captain and was firmly established as England's number three, but his patience was over-taxed in Pakistan and he lost the captaincy. He was a victim of the pernicious practice of planting a microphone behind the stumps and an altercation with an umpire was relayed to the world. Such are the pitfalls of international captaincy today.

In 1989 Middlesex were defeated in the NatWest Trophy final at Lord's thanks to a lusty final blow from Neil Smith of Warwickshire. A year later, however, in 1990, the men from St John's Wood tied up the county championship and the Refuge Assurance Cup, beating Derbyshire in the final at Edgbaston. Many of these achievements were thanks to the fine batting of Desmond Haynes and Mike Gatting.

The Sunday League was won for the first and only time in 1992 when Yorkshire were beaten at Uxbridge. The county championship was last won in 1993. The departure of John Carr, Roland Butcher, Simon Hughes and Paul Downton through an injury suffered from a flying bail has left a gap. However, Middlesex have filled these positions with the likes of Mark Ramprakash, Paul Weekes, Phil Tufnell, Owais Shah, Richard Johnson and David Nash.

The retirement of Don Bennett as coach in 1997 brought in the Australian John Buchanan, but his presence did not bring the immediate success that he had achieved with Queensland in the Sheffield Shield.

Middlesex Players celebrating Denis Compton's seventieth birthday. Left to right: Wayne Daniel, Norman Cowans, Bill Edrich, Denis Compton, Mike Gatting and Roland Butcher.

Since the departure of Desmond Haynes, three useful young international cricketers have filled the overseas position: all-rounder Dion Nash of New Zealand between 1995 and 1996, although he was dogged by injury, the impressive Jacques Kallis of South Africa in 1997 and the left-handed top order Australian batsman Justin Langer in 1998. Mark Ramprakash took over the captaincy of the county from Mike Gatting in 1997. Gatting fell short of that elusive hundred first-class centuries, deciding to retire at the end of 1998 to become county coach.

This introduction cannot be concluded without my thanking first John Warr for his foreword to this photographic history of Middlesex County Cricket Club and secondly the many who have assisted me with this work – all those who have made some contribution are included in the acknowledgements. For current players, all statistics are up to and including the end of the 1998 English season.

William A. Powell
Hemel Hempstead
Hertfordshire
January 1999

CHAPTER ONE

EARLY DAYS & THE WALKER BROTHERS

Vyell Walker (1859–77). Born in Southgate, Middlesex, in 1837, Vyell Walker was a right-handed middle-order batsman, who played 52 matches for Middlesex, accumulating 1,310 runs (av. 17.70) with a top score of 87 not out versus Surrey at the Oval in 1867. As a right-hand slow under-arm bowler, he took 120+ 10 wicket hauls (av. 15.13) with a best performance of 10 for 104 versus Lancashire at Old Trafford in 1865, and was an excellent fieldsman who held 84 catches. He attended Harrow School before representing Middlesex in 52 matches between 1859 and 1877, and he also played one season of minor county cricket with Bedfordshire in 1863. In 1860 he was the best all-round amateur cricketer in England and in 1859 at the Oval scored 108 and took 14 for 91 for England versus Surrey. He captained the county from 1864 to 1872 and was President of the MCC in 1891. He had been Middlesex Treasurer from 1897 and President in 1869, and again from 1898 until his death in 1906 at Arnos Grove, Middlesex.

Russell Walker (1862–77). Born in Southgate, Middlesex, in 1842, Russell Walker, brother of Alfred (Middlesex), A.H. (Middlesex), Frederic (Middlesex), John (Middlesex), Isaac D. (Middlesex) and Vyell E. (Middlesex), nephew of Henry (MCC, 1832) was a right-handed attacking opening batsman, right-hand slow round-arm bowler and good fieldsman. He attended Harrow School and then went on to Oxford University where he attained blues all five years between 1861 and 1865. He represented Middlesex 45 times between 1862 and 1877 during which time he amassed 1,678 runs (av. 22.07) with a highest score of 104 versus Surrey at the Oval in 1876, his only century. He bagged 142 wickets (av. 17.54) with a best performance of 6 for 76 and held 36 catches. His best season was 1865 when he recorded 770 runs (av. 24.83); his last first-class match was for the MCC in 1878. He was a committee member of both the MCC and Middlesex until his death, having served as President of Middlesex from 1906 to 1922 and as a Trustee of the MCC. He represented Oxford University at rackets, being a notable player. He died at Regent's Park, London, in 1922.

Isaac Walker (1862–84). Born in Southgate, Middlesex, in 1844, Isaac Walker was a right-handed stylish middle-order batsman, right-hand fast, later slow, under-arm bowler and excellent deep fieldsman. He attended Harrow School prior to joining Middlesex in 1862 and represented the county 144 times until his retirement in 1884. He accumulated 6,065 runs (av. 25.48) including four centuries with a top score of 145 versus Gloucestershire at Clifton College in 1883, he took 152 wickets (av. 20.73) with a best performance of 6 for 42 and held 138 catches. His best season was 1868 when he scored 661 runs (av. 34.78). He captained the county from 1873 to 1884 and continued as a committee member until his death. He had been associated with the county club since its foundation in 1864, and scored 102 on his county debut versus Surrey Club at the Oval in 1862. He died at Regent's Park, London, in 1898.

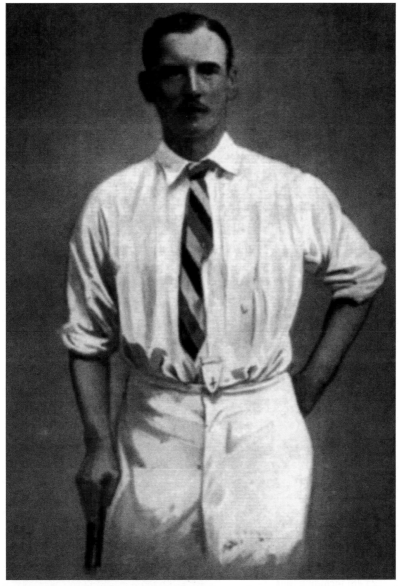

Alexander Webbe (1875–1900). Born in Bethnal Green, London, in 1855, brother of H.R. (Middlesex) and G.A. (MCC), Alexander Webbe was a stylish right-handed opening batsman, right-arm fast-medium bowler, specialist mid-wicket fieldsman and occasional wicket-keeper. Educated at Harrow, he went on to Oxford University attaining blues all four years between 1875 and 1878 and captained the side in 1877 and 1878. He represented the county 247 times between 1875 and 1900. For Middlesex he scored 9,405 runs (av. 24.33) with 7 centuries, bagged 68 wickets (av. 29.25) and he held 149 catches and took 6 stumpings. During his career he scored 14,465 runs (av. 24.81) with 14 centuries including a top score of 243 not out versus Yorkshire at Huddersfield in 1897. He bagged 109 wickets (av. 25.21) with a best haul of 5 for 23, and he held 228 catches and took 10 stumpings. His best season was 1887 when he recorded 1,244 runs (av. 47.84). He captained Middlesex between 1885 and 1898, being joint leader with Andrew Stoddart in 1898. He acted as Middlesex Secretary between 1900 and 1922 and was club President during the period 1923–36. A useful rackets player and footballer, he represented Oxford University in both sports. He died at Fulvens, Hoe, Abinger Hammer, Surrey, in 1941.

The 1876 team. Back: Howitt (umpire). Back row, left to right: M. Flanagan, A. Burghes, C.J. Lucas, M. Turner, R. Henderson, C.F. Butler. Front row: W.H. Hadow, A.J. Webbe, I.D. Walker (captain), J.W. Dale, H.R. Webbe.

Sir Timothy O'Brien (1881–98). Born in Dublin in 1861, Timothy O'Brien, brother of J.G. (Ireland) and brother-in-law of C.E. de Trafford (Warwickshire and Leicestershire) was an attractive middle-order right-handed batsman and useful left-arm bowler. He attended Downside School before going on to Oxford University, where he attained blues in 1884 and 1885. O'Brien represented Middlesex in 156 matches between 1881 and 1898 scoring 7,377 runs (av. 29.62) including ten centuries, with a top score of 202 versus Sussex at Hove in 1895. He also took 2 wickets (av. 136.00) with a best of 1 for 10, held 111 catches and took 2 stumpings. He hit 1,000 runs in a season on three occasions with a best of 1,150 (av. 27.38) in 1884. Playing 5 Tests for England, one as captain, between 1884 and 1895/96, he scored 59 runs (av. 7.37) with a highest score of 20 and he held 4 catches. He toured overseas twice: with Vernon to Australia in 1887/88 and Lord Hawke to South Africa in 1895/96. He also represented Ireland in first-class matches between 1902 and 1907. O'Brien became Sir Timothy after succeeding to a baronetcy on the death of his uncle. His last first-class match was for L. Robinson's XI when he scored 90 and 111 in 1914. He died at Ramsay, Isle of Man, in 1948.

Andrew Stoddart (1885–1900). Born in Westoe, South Shields, Co. Durham, Stoddart joined Middlesex in 1885 from Hampstead CC, where he had recorded 485 in 370 minutes, out of Hampstead's total of 813 versus Stoics. He played for the county until 1900 as a stylish right-handed batsman, right-arm medium-pace bowler and fine fieldsman. He played 170 matches for Middlesex accumulating 9,255 runs (av. 31.80) with 16 centuries and a top score of 221 versus Somerset at Lord's in 1900. He took 141 wickets (av. 28.63) with a best of 5 for 78 and held 156 catches. Playing 309 first-class matches during his career, he scored 16,738 runs with 26 centuries, he took 278 wickets and held 257 catches. Playing 16 Tests for England he amassed 996 runs with a top score of 173 versus Australia at Melbourne in 1894/95, which until 1974/75 was the highest score by an England captain in Australia. He captained and organised two of his four tours abroad and he was the first England captain to ask the opposition to bat in a Test Match. He was acknowledged as the best rugby three-quarter of his day in England, and he captained his country several times in his ten internationals. He died at St John's Wood, London, in 1915 by his own hand.

The 1884 team. Back row, left to right: G. Burton, Sir T.C. O'Brien, J.E.K. Studd, W.C. Clarke. Front row: P.J. de Paravicini, T.S. Pearson, Hon. A. Lyttleton, I.D. Walker (captain), A.J. Webbe, J. Robertson, G.F. Vernon.

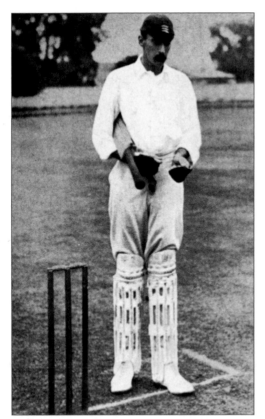

Francis Ford (1886–99). Born in Paddington, London, in 1866, Francis Ford was son of W.A. (MCC, 1839), brother of A.F.J. (Middlesex) and W.J. (Middlesex), nephew of G.J. (Oxford University), uncle of N.M. (Derbyshire and Middlesex) and great-uncle of J.R.T. Barclay (Sussex). An attractive left-handed middle-order batsman, slow left-arm bowler and excellent slip fieldsman, he attended Repton School before going to Cambridge University. He attained blues all four years between 1887 and 1890 and captained the side in 1889. He made his Middlesex debut in 1886 and represented the county in 102 matches until 1899. For Middlesex he amassed 4,650 runs (av. 28.88) with 10 centuries and a top score of 160 versus Sussex at Lord's in 1898. He hit 1,000 runs in a season twice with a best of 1,195 (av. 28.45) in 1899. He bagged 87 wickets (av. 25.18) with a best of 6 for 56 and held 72 catches. He played 5 Tests for England in Australia in 1894/95 when he toured with Stoddart's team scoring 48 runs (av. 18.66) and taking a single wicket. His final first-class match was for an England XI in 1908. A noted goalkeeper, he was awarded a blue for soccer while at Cambridge. He died at Burwash, Sussex, in 1940.

J.T. 'Jack' Hearne (1888–1923). Born in Chalfont St Giles, Buckinghamshire, in 1867, 'Jack' Hearne was an outstanding right-arm medium-pace bowler and after being summoned by telegram to play in his first championship match at Lord's, he took six Nottinghamshire wickets. Representing Middlesex 453 times from 1888 until 1923, he collected 2,093 wickets (av. 18.23) with a best of 9 for 32 versus Nottinghamshire at Trent Bridge in 1891. He recorded 5 wickets in an innings 171 times and 10 wickets in a match 30 times. He scored 4,598 runs (av. 11.29) with a highest score of 65 and held 310 catches mainly at slip. He was cousin of the three Hearne brothers who represented Kent, and 'Young Jack' of Middlesex. He was the first player to achieve 100 wickets in a season: this was on 12 June 1896. He topped 100 wickets in a season on fifteen occasions and he achieved 200 wickets in a season three times. As a Test player his highlight in 12 Tests was taking a hat trick versus Australia at Headingley in 1899 when he dismissed Clem Hill, Syd Gregory and Monty Noble, all for ducks. He later acted as coach for Oxford University and the Maharaja of Patiala in India before being elected one of the first professionals to the club committee; he died at his birthplace in 1944.

J.T. Rawlin (1889–1909). A right-arm fast-medium bowler and right-handed lower order batsman, John Rawlin, father of E.R. (Yorkshire) was born in Greasborough, Rotherham, Yorkshire, in 1856. He represented his native Yorkshire twenty-seven times between 1880 and 1885 before moving south to represent Middlesex in 229 matches between 1889 and 1909. He bagged 659 wickets (av. 20.14) with a best haul of 8 for 29 versus Gloucestershire at Bristol in 1893. He took 5 wickets in an innings 35 times and 10 wickets in a match 11 times, and held 159 catches. His best season was 1894 when he achieved 104 wickets (av. 14.53). He scored 5,680 runs (av. 17.57), with a single three-figure score of 100 against arch rivals from south of the River Thames, Surrey, at the Oval in 1901. He held 159 catches and despite not playing Test cricket for England, in 1887/88 he toured Australia with G.F. Vernon's XI. He died at his place of birth in 1924.

The 1891 team. Back row, left to right: J.T. Rawlin, J.T. Hearne, J. Phillips. Middle row: E.M. Hadow, T.C. O'Brien, A.J. Webbe (captain), J.E. West, S.W. Scott. Front row: A.E. Stoddart, E.A. Nepean, P.J.T. Henery.

R. Slade Lucas (1891–1900). Born in Teddington, Middlesex, in 1867, Slade Lucas learnt his early cricket while at Merchant Taylors' School. A right-handed middle-order batsman and right-arm medium pace bowler he represented Middlesex in 73 matches between 1891 and 1900. For the county he scored 2,064 runs (av. 18.26) with a single century of 185 versus Sussex at Brighton in 1895, took 3 wickets (av. 57.00) with a best of 2 for 44 and held 33 catches. During his career he accumulated 2,685 runs (av. 18.64) with one century, and took 6 wickets (av. 61.00) with a best of 2 for 44. He also held 42 catches. He toured overseas twice with Lord Hawke to North America in 1894 and with his own side to the West Indies in 1894/95, which was the first by an English touring team. A well-respected hockey player, he was captain of Teddington Hockey Club for many seasons. He died at Franklands Village, Haywards Heath, Sussex, in 1942.

The 1892 team. Back row, left to right: R.S. Lucas, W.R. Collins, T.C. O'Brien, F.G.J. Ford, A.E. Stoddart, J.T. Hearne. Front row: P.J.T. Henery, J. Phillips, A.J. Webbe (captain), J.T. Rawlin, G. MacGregor.

MIDDLESEX

A.E.Stoddart

P. F. Warner

B.J.T.Bosanquet.

F.A.Tarrant

C.C.Page

A.J.Webbe

J. T. Rawlin

MIDDLESEX

Greg.rMacGregor

Francis G. J. Ford

H.B.Hayman.

George Burton

J. T. Hearne

A. E. Trott

J.D.Walker

Middlesex cricketers' autographs, 1890 to 1910. This interesting collection includes G. MacGregor, F.G.J. Ford, H.B. Hayman, G. Burton, A.E. Stoddart, P.F. Warner, B.J.T. Bosanquet, F.A. Tarrant, C.C. Page, A.J. Webbe, J.T. Rawlin, J.T. Hearne, A.E. Trott and J.D. Walker.

Gregor MacGregor (1892–1907). Born in Edinburgh in 1869, MacGregor was a lower-order, right-handed batsman and wicket-keeper. After attending Uppingham School he went on to Cambridge, attaining blues between 1888 and 1891. He made his Middlesex debut versus Lancashire in 1892, representing the county in 184 matches until 1907. For Middlesex he accumulated 4,846 runs (av. 19.61) with two centuries and a top score of 141 versus Sussex at Lord's in 1897; he held 280 catches and took 111 stumpings. He played 8 Tests for England between 1890 and 1893 scoring 96 runs (av. 12.00) with a top score of 31, and took 14 catches and 3 stumpings. He toured overseas twice with Lord Sheffield to Australia in 1891/92 and with the MCC to North America in 1907. He captained Cambridge in 1891 and Middlesex from 1899 to 1907. A brilliant rugby player at full-back and centre, he represented Cambridge in the Varsity matches of 1889 and 1890 and between these years represented Scotland in thirteen internationals. In 1890 he scored 131 out of a total of 730 for 9 declared by Cambridge University against Sussex at Hove which was the highest second innings total in a first-class match in England. In his first season as Middlesex skipper, Somerset were defeated in just 4 hours and 15 minutes. He was a Test selector in 1902 and from 1916 until his death was Honorary Treasurer. He died at Marylebone in 1919.

Sir Pelham Warner (1894–1920). Born in Trinidad in 1873 and coached by Tom Emmett, 'Plum' Warner captained Rugby School before making his first-class debut for Oxford University in 1894, where he gained blues in 1895 and 1896. A right-handed batsman, he played for Middlesex 345 times from 1894 to 1920, acting as captain between 1908 and 1920. For the county he scored 19,507 runs (av. 37.44) with 46 centuries and 94 half-centuries, with a highest innings of 197 not out versus Somerset at Lord's in 1901. He took 4 wickets (av. 49.50) with a best of 1 for 4 and held 123 catches. Playing 519 first-class matches, during his career he scored 29,028 runs with 60 centuries, and recorded a top score of 244 for the Rest of England versus Warwickshire at the Oval in 1911. For England he played 15 Tests from 1898/99 to 1912 and scored 622 runs with a best of 132 not out versus South Africa at Johannesburg in 1898/99. Few have dedicated so much of their life to the game as 'Plum' in his capacity as player, manager, Test selector, writer and founder of The Cricketer magazine in 1921. In 1937 he was knighted for his services to cricket. He acted as deputy secretary of the MCC during the Second World War and became President in 1950/51. A stand at Lord's was named after him in 1958. He died at West Lavington, Sussex, in 1953, and his ashes were scattered at Lord's, near the spot where he hit his first four.

Cyril Wells (1895-1909). Born in St Pancras, London, in 1871, brother of L.S. (Middlesex) and Clifford (Cambridge University), Cyril Wells was an attractive right-handed middle-order batsman, off- and leg-break bowler and fine slip fieldsman. Schooled at Dulwich, he attained blues all three years between 1891 and 1893 while at Cambridge University. He played four matches for Surrey between 1892 and 1893 before moving to Lord's in 1895. He represented Middlesex 113 times between 1895 and 1909, and for the club he scored 3,383 runs (av. 23.82) with four centuries, bagged 350 wickets (av. 20.52) and held 83 catches. During his career he accumulated 4,229 runs (av. 22.02) with four centuries including a top score of 244 for Middlesex versus Nottinghamshire at Trent Bridge in 1899. Wells bagged 465 wickets (av. 19.86) with a best performance of 8 for 35, and held 122 catches. A well-respected rugby player, he represented Cambridge University, Harlequins, Middlesexand England. He died at St John's Wood, London, in 1963.

The 1896 team. Back row, left to right: E.H. Bray, J. Phillips, J.T. Rawlin. Middle row: J.T. Hearne, A.E. Stoddart, A.J. Webbe (captain), T.C. O'Brien, R.S. Lucas. Front row: P.F. Warner, R.W. Nicholls, H.R. Bromley-Davenport.

Albert Trott (1898–1910). Born in Melbourne, Australia, in 1873, a class all-rounder, Albert Trott represented his native Victoria and Australia before joining Middlesex, having been excluded from the Australian touring party. He scored 72 and took 8 for 43 in his first Test versus England at Adelaide, and qualified to play for the county between 1898 and 1910. For Middlesex he played 323 matches taking 946 wickets (av. 21.49) with a best of 10 for 42 versus Somerset at Taunton in 1900. He recorded 5 wickets in an innings 71 times and 10 wickets in a match 23 times. He scored 6,253 runs (av. 20.33) with 6 centuries with a top score of 164 versus Yorkshire at Lord's in 1899, and held 253 catches. During his career he played 375 first-class matches, scored 10,696 runs, achieved 1,674 wickets and held 452 catches. Playing for the MCC versus the touring Australians at Lord's in 1899 he hit a ball bowled by Monty Noble clean over the roof of the members' pavilion. In 1899 and 1900 he achieved the double of 1,000 runs and 200 wickets in a season. He also represented London County CC from 1900 to 1904 and Hawke's Bay in New Zealand in 1901/02. He played a total of 5 Tests, 3 for Australia in 1894/95 versus England and 2 for England in 1898/99 versus South Africa, scoring a total of 228 runs and taking 26 wickets. He later acted as an umpire from 1911 to 1913 and after suffering from dropsy he took his own life in 1914 at his lodgings in Willesden Green, north-west London.

Bernard Bosanquet (1898–1919). Born in Bulls Cross, Enfield, in 1877, Bernard Bosanquet was a tall medium-pace right-arm leg-break bowler who invented the googly, and a hard-hitting batsman. He represented Oxford University from 1898 to 1900 and Middlesex between 1898 and 1919, playing 123 first-class matches. He accumulated 6,593 runs (av. 35.25) with 13 centuries and a highest score of 179, bagged 268 wickets (av. 27.13) with a best of 8 for 53 and held 91 catches. During his career he scored 11,696 runs with 21 centuries and took 629 wickets. He achieved the coveted double in 1904 and became the first to complete a match double of a century in each innings and an aggregate of 10 wickets in the same match versus Sussex at Lord's in 1905. He hit 214 in 195 minutes while playing for the Rest of England versus Yorkshire at the Oval in 1908. Playing 7 Tests for England between 1903/04 and 1905, he took 25 wickets with a best performance of 8 for 107 versus Australia at Trent Bridge in 1905. He toured overseas three times, and while at university he gained half-blues at billiards and hammer throwing and was also a fine ice hockey player. Father of the late Reginald Bosanquet of television news fame, he died at Ewhurst, Surrey, in 1936.

CHAPTER TWO

THE GOLDEN AGE

The 1901 team. Back row, left to right: J.T. Hearne, B.J.T. Bosanquet, G.W. Beldam, A.E. Trott, J.T. Rawlin. Middle row: C.M. Wells, J. Douglas, G. MacGregor (captain), R.N. Douglas, P.F. Warner. Front row: W.P. Robinson, R.E. More.

George Beldam (1900–07). Born in New Cross, Kent, in 1868, George was the cousin of C.A. and E.A. Beldam, who also represented Middlesex. A sound right-handed middle-order batsman and right-arm medium slow bowler, he represented the county in 102 first-class matches between 1900 and 1907. For Middlesex he scored 4,796 runs (av. 30.16) with 7 centuries, and a top score of 155 not out. He took 76 wickets (av. 27.14) with a best of 5 for 28 and held 66 catches. During his career he scored 6,562 first-class runs (av. 30.23) with 9 centuries; his top score was 155 not out versus Surrey at Lord's in 1903. He bagged 107 wickets (av. 30.63) with a best performance of 5 for 28 and held 83 catches. He scored 1,000 runs in a season on three occasions with a best of 1,158 (av. 38.60) in 1901. The pioneer of action photography, he produced the plate photographs for the remarkable *Great Batsmen and Great Bowlers, Their Methods at a Glance* books published in 1907. He also wrote books on golf and tennis. He died in 1937 at Lower Bourne, Surrey.

The 1902 team. Back row, left to right: J.T. Hearne, R.W. Nicholls, B.J.T. Bosanquet, J.T. Rawlin. Middle row: L.J. Moon, C.M. Wells, G. MacGregor (captain), P.F. Warner, G.W. Beldam. Front row: J. Douglas, A.E. Trott, E.A. Beldam.

The 1903 Championship winning team. Back row, left to right: J.T. Rawlin, J.H. Hunt, A.E. Trott, E.A. Beldam, J. T. Hearne. Middle row: B.J.T. Bosanquet, P.F. Warner, G. MacGregor (captain), C.M. Wells, G.W. Beldam. Front row: J. Douglas, L.J. Moon.

The 1904 team. Back row, left to right: J.T. Hearne, C. Palmer, P.F. Warner, J.H. Stogdon, R.E. More. Middle row: B.J.T. Bosanquet, J. Douglas, G. MacGregor (captain), G.W. Beldam, C.M. Wells. Front row: E. Mignon, A.E. Trott.

Frank Tarrant (1904–14). Born in Fitzroy, Melbourne, Australia, in 1880, the father of L.B. (Australians in India) and nephew of W.A. (Victoria), Frank Tarrant was a right-handed middle-order batsman, left-arm slow-medium bowler and an excellent slip fieldsman. He represented his native Victoria 13 times between 1898/99 to 1925/26 and played 206 times for Middlesex between 1904 and 1914. For the county he accumulated 12,169 runs (av. 38.02) with 26 centuries, including a highest score of 250 not out versus Essex at Leyton in 1914; he bagged 1,005 wickets (av. 17.43) with a best performance of 9 for 41 versus Gloucestershire at Bristol in 1907 and held 193 catches. He hit 1,000 runs in a season nine times, going on to 2,000 once in 1911, when he hit 2,030 (av. 46.13). He exceeded 100 wickets in a season eight times with a best of 183 (av. 15.70) in 1907. Regarded as the best all-rounder of his time, he achieved the coveted double eight times. Tarrant toured India with an Australian XI but never played Test cricket. He played matches for the Europeans between 1915/16 and 1936/37 and Patiala's XI between 1926/27 and 1933/34. In 1918/19 while playing for the Maharaja of Cooch Behar's XI at Poona in India he took 10 for 90 and hit 182 not out in the same match. He umpired a single Test in 1933/34 and died at Upper Hawthorn, Melbourne, in 1951.

Harry Murrell (1905–26). Born in Hounslow, Middlesex, in 1879, Harry Murrell was a right-handed lower-order batsman, left-arm bowler and wicket-keeper. He made his first-class debut for Kent in 1899 and represented them in 27 matches until 1905. During the 1905 season he moved from Canterbury to Lord's, and represented Middlesex from 1905 until 1926 on 342 occasions. For the county he scored 6,033 runs (av. 14.75), recorded 20 half-centuries with a top score of 96 not out, held 517 catches and took 261 stumpings. During his career he accumulated 6,663 runs (av. 14.29) with a top score of 96 not out, held 565 catches and took 269 stumpings. A useful footballer, he appeared for Arsenal. He was Middlesex scorer from 1946 until he died at West Wickham, Kent, in 1952.

Albert Vogler (1906). Born in Swartwater, South Africa, in 1876, Vogler was a leg-break and googly bowler and right-handed middle-order batsman. He represented Middlesex in a single match versus Cambridge University at Fenner's in 1906 while a member of the Lord's groundstaff, with the intention of qualifying to represent the county, but he returned to South Africa. He scored 87 runs (av. 43.50) with a top score of 52 and took 5 wickets (av. 18.20) with a best bowling performance of 4 for 71. He played the rest of his first-class cricket for Natal in 1903/04, Transvaal between 1904/05 and 1909/10 and Western Province between 1905/06 and 1906/07. He played 15 Tests for South Africa between 1905/06 and 1910/11 and toured abroad twice, to England in 1907 and to Australia in 1910/11. He scored 340 runs (av. 17.00) with a top score of 65 and bagged 64 wickets (av. 22.73) including a best haul of 7 for 94. His best bowling performance was 10 for 26 for Eastern Province versus Griqualand West at Johannesburg in 1906/07. His final first-class match was in South Africa for L.J. Tancred's XI in 1911/12. He died at Fort Napier, Pietermaritzburg, South Africa, in 1946.

Mr E.S. Littlejohn   E. Mignon

Some Taddy County Cricketers cigarette cards issued depicting Middlesex cricketers, 1907.

Mr G.G. Napier   Mr C.C. Page

Mr M.W. Payne

Mr E.A. Beldam

Mr James Douglas

J.T. Hearne

The 1907 team. Back row, left to right: E. Mignon, A.E. Trott, F.A. Tarrant, W.P. Harrison. Middle row: P.F. Warner, G.W. Beldham, G. MacGregor (captain), E.S. Littlejohn, C.C. Page. Front row: J.T. Hearne, H.R. Murrell.

Elias 'Patsy' Hendren (1907–37). 'Patsy' was born in Turnham Green in 1889, and joined the Lord's groundstaff in 1905. A right-handed batsman, he represented Middlesex from 1907 to 1937 playing 581 matches, scoring 40,302 runs (av. 49.81) with 71 centuries and 115 half-centuries, and a top score of 301 not out versus Worcestershire at Dudley in 1933. He took 39 wickets (av. 52.94) with a best of 5 for 43 and held 561 catches. Playing 833 first-class matches during his career, he scored a mammoth 57,611 runs (av. 50.80) with 170 centuries. His top score was 301 not out and he also held 754 catches. He exceeded 1,000 runs in a season 21 times and holds the county record for the most runs in a season: 2,669 in 1923. Playing 51 Tests for England between 1920/21 and 1934/35 he amassed 3,525 runs with a top score of 205 not out versus West Indies at Port of Spain in 1929/30. After retiring he coached at Harrow School and later for Sussex, and was Middlesex county scorer between 1952 and 1960. A notable footballer, he played wing forward for Brentford, Queen's Park Rangers, Manchester City and Coventry City. He died at Tooting Bec, London, in 1962.

The 1908 team. Back row, left to right: E. Mignon, C. Palmer, A.R. Littlejohn, A.E. Trott, J.T. Hearne, F.A. Tarrant. Front row: B.J.T. Bosanquet, P.F. Warner, G. MacGregor (captain), C.M. Wells, J. Douglas.

The Hon. Clarence Bruce (1908–29). Born in London in 1885, Bruce succeeded to the title 3rd Baron Aberdare in 1929. A right-handed, hard-hitting middle-order batsman he attended Winchester School before university. He represented Oxford University from 1905 to 1908, attaining blues in 1907 and 1908. He made his Middlesex debut in 1908 and played 62 times for the county until 1929. For Middlesex he accumulated 2,959 runs (av. 32.16) with 3 centuries with a top score of 149, and held 19 catches. During his career he scored 4,326 runs (av. 29.03) with a top score of 149, and held 34 catches. An excellent rackets player, he was amateur champion in 1922 and 1931 and doubles champion on ten occasions. He represented Oxford University at both rackets and golf and for over twenty years worked for the International Olympic Executive. He also played cricket for Wales from 1925 to 1929. He died in 1957, near Kotor in Yugoslavia, where he was drowned after the car in which he was travelling went over a precipice into a river.

The 1909 team. Back row, left to right: E. Mignon. J.H. Hunt, H.R. Murrell, A.R. Littlejohn, F.A. Tarrant, A.E. Trott. Front row: C.C. Page, E.S. Littlejohn, P.F. Warner (captain), L.J. Moon, J.T. Hearne.

Frank Mann (1909–31). Born in Winchmore Hill, Middlesex, in 1888, Frank Mann learnt his cricket at Malvern in Worcestershire before playing for Cambridge University from 1908 to 1911. A lusty right-handed batsman and occasional right-arm slow bowler, he represented Middlesex 314 times from 1909 to 1931 (1921 to 1928 as captain), winning a famous championship at his first attempt in 1921. He scored 10,656 runs (av. 24.60) with 8 centuries with a top score of 194, took 2 wickets (av. 86.00) with a best of 1 for 15 and held 137 catches for the county. He played 398 first-class matches during his career, scoring 13,235 runs with 9 centuries and with a top score of 194. Captaining England in his 5 Tests versus South Africa in 1922/23, he won 14 of the 22 tour matches including the Test series 2-1, with wins at Cape Town and Durban. He scored 281 runs with a top score of 84 in the third Test at Durban. In 1930 he became a Test selector and subsequently President of the club. He died at Milton-Lilbourne, Wiltshire, in 1964.

J.W. Hearne (1909–36). 'Young Jack' Hearne joined the groundstaff at Lord's in 1906 as a scorecard boy and developed into a fine right-handed all-rounder. He represented Middlesex 465 times from 1909 to 1936 scoring 27,612 runs (av. 41.15) with 71 centuries and 115 half-centuries with a top score of 285 not out versus Essex at the County Ground, Leyton, in 1929. He bagged 1,438 wickets (av. 23.15) with a best of 9 for 61. He recorded 5 wickets in an innings 88 times and 10 wickets in a match 17 times and held 240 catches. He played 647 first-class matches during his career, accumulating 37,252 runs with 96 centuries, and recorded a top score of 285 not out. That innings was the last of his eleven double centuries for the county. He took 1,839 wickets with a best performance of 9 for 61 and held 348 catches. Playing 24 Tests for England between 1911/12 and 1926, he scored 806 runs with a top score of 114 versus Australia at Melbourne in 1911/12 and took 30 wickets with a best return of 5 for 49 versus South Africa at Johannesburg in 1913/14. He accumulated 1,000 runs in a season nineteen times and achieved the coveted double five times. But for the First World War he would easily have achieved 100 first-class centuries. He later owned a sports shop, and he died at West Drayton, Middlesex, in 1965.

Harry Lee (1911–34). Born in Marylebone, London, in 1890, Harry was the brother of F.S. (Middlesex and Somerset) and J.W. (Middlesex and Somerset). A solid right-handed opening batsman and right-arm slow-medium off-break bowler, he represented Middlesex 401 times between 1911 and 1934. He amassed 18,594 runs (av. 29.94) with 35 centuries, and with a top score of 243 not out versus Nottinghamshire at Lord's in 1921. He hit 1,000 runs in a season thirteen times with a best of 1,995 (av. 37.64) in 1929. He bagged 240 wickets (av. 32.54) with a best performance of 8 for 39 versus Gloucestershire at Cheltenham College in 1923 and held 164 catches. While coaching in South Africa in 1930/31 he was co-opted to the England touring party and played in a single Test for England, scoring 19 runs in two innings (av. 9.50). He played winter cricket in India in 1917/18 for Cooch-Behar's XI and for an England XI in 1918/19. He later became a first-class umpire, standing between 1935 and 1946, and later coached at Downside School from 1949 to 1953. He also wrote the book *Forty Years of English Cricket*. He died at Westminster, London, in 1981.

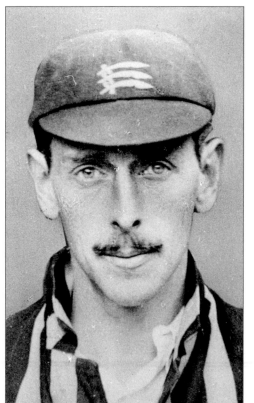

Nigel Haig (1912–34). Born in Kensington, London, in 1887, Haig was the nephew of Lord Harris (Kent). A right-handed middle-order batsman, right-arm medium-fast bowler and good fieldsman he was educated at Eton. He represented Middlesex 417 times between 1912 and 1934, scored 12,289 runs (av. 20.79) with 11 centuries and a top score of 131 versus Sussex at Lord's in 1920. He achieved 931 wickets (av. 26.06) with a best of 7 for 33 versus Kent at Canterbury in 1920 and held 182 catches. He hit 1,000 runs in a season six times with a best of 1,552 (av. 25.02) in 1929, and took 100 wickets in a season five times collecting 129 (av. 24.17) in 1929. He achieved the coveted double three times. He represented England in 5 Tests in 1929/30 when he toured with the MCC to the West Indies. He took 13 wickets (av. 34.46) with a best of 3 for 73 and scored 126 runs (av. 14.00) with a top score of 47 and held 4 catches. Between 1929 and 1934 he captained the county, the latter two seasons jointly with H.J. Enthoven, and was also Honorary Secretary. He played three other sports to a high standard: tennis, rackets and golf. He was a Test selector in 1929 and made his final first-class appearance in 1936 for H.D.G. Leveson-Gower's XI. He died at Eastbourne in 1966.

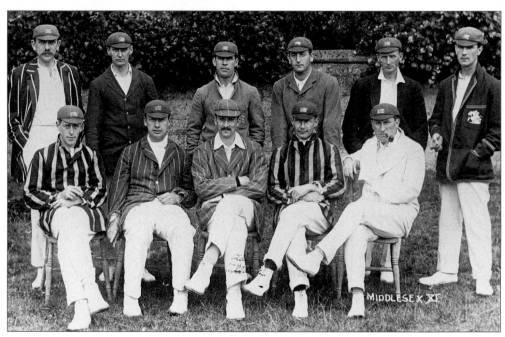

The 1914 team. Back row, left to right: J.T. Hearne, H.R. Murrell, E.H. Hendren, F.A. Tarrant, P. Clarke, J.W. Hearne. Front row: N.E. Haig, F.T. Mann, E.L. Kidd, W.P. Robertson, E.S. Littlejohn.

Jack Durston (1919–33). Born in Clophill, Bedfordshire, in 1893, Jack Durston was a right-arm fast bowler, latterly medium pace, and a useful lower-order hard-hitting right-handed batsman. He represented Middlesex 349 times from 1919 to 1933 taking 1,178 wickets (av. 21.96) with a best performance of 8 for 27, and recorded 5 wickets in an innings 65 times. He scored 3,569 runs (av. 11.62) with a top score of 92 not out versus Northamptonshire at Lord's in 1930 and held 230 catches. He took 100 wickets in a season on six occasions with a best of 136 (av. 19.50) in 1921. He toured abroad twice with Cahn to Jamaica in 1928/29 and with Brinckman to South America in 1937/38. He played a single Test for England against Australia in 1921 when he took 5 wickets (av. 27.20) and scored 8 runs. At 6 feet 5 inches tall he was a more than useful goalkeeper for Brentford. He died at Norwood Green, Southall, Middlesex, in 1965.

The 1919 team. Back row, left to right: F.J. Durston, C.H. Gunasekera, H.R. Murrell, J.W. Hearne, E.H. Hendren, H.W. Lee. Front row: N.E. Haig, F.T. Mann, P.F. Warner (captain), Hon. C.N. Bruce, G.E.V. Crutchley.

Greville Stevens (1919–32). Born in Hampstead, London, in 1901, Greville Stevens was a right-handed middle-order batsman, leg-break bowler and good close fieldsman. He attended University College School and Oxford University where he attained blues all four years between 1920 and 1923. He represented Middlesex 127 times between 1919 and 1932, during which time he accumulated 5,434 runs (av. 30.18) with seven centuries including a highest score of 170 not out. He bagged 385 wickets (av. 27.41) with a best haul of 8 for 38 and held 107 catches. He hit 1,000 runs in a season twice with a best of 1,434 (av. 33.34) in 1923. In 1919 while playing in a house match at school he hit 466, and immediately afterwards was selected to play for the Gentlemen versus Players at Lord's. He captained Oxford University in his last year – 1923 – but he could never spare the time to play for Middlesex regularly. He played 10 Tests for England between 1922/23 and 1929/30, accumulated 263 runs (av. 15.47) and took 20 wickets (av. 32.40) with a best of 5 for 90. He toured overseas four times with the MCC to South Africa in 1922/23 and 1927/28, West Indies 1929/30 and with Lord Tennyson's XI to Jamaica in 1931/32. His final first-class match was for the MCC versus H.D.G. Leveson-Gower's XI in 1933. He died at Islington, London, in 1970.

CHAPTER THREE

CHAMPIONS & TWENTIES

Championship winning team, 1920. Back row, left to right: H.W. Lee, H.K. Longman, F. J. Durston, N.E. Haig, G.T.S. Stevens, C.H.L. Skeet. Front row: J.W. Hearne, F.T. Mann, P.F. Warner (captain), H.R. Murrell, E.H. Hendren.

Pelham Warner is chaired off the field at Lord's Cricket Ground after he had led Middlesex to victory over arch rivals Surrey (and with it the County Championship) at 6.22 p.m. on 31 August 1920.

County record. Middlesex established a county record versus Sussex at Lord's in May 1920, when the first four batsmen scored centuries. Left to right: P.F. Warner (139), H.W. Lee (119), J.W. Hearne (116 not out), and N.E. Haig (131).

Sir George Allen CBE, TD (1921–50). A powerful influence on the game of cricket and a major force at Lord's for over sixty years as a high-class all-rounder, captain, selector and administrator, Sir George 'Gubby' Allen was born in Bellevue Hill, Sydney, in 1902. He represented Middlesex in 146 first-class matches from 1921 to 1950 and Cambridge University in 1922 and 1923. For Middlesex he accumulated 4,667 runs (av. 25.64) with 4 centuries with a top score of 155, bagged 420 wickets (av. 20.64) with a best of 10 for 40 (8 clean bowled) versus Lancashire at Lord's in 1929, and held 56 catches. Representing his country in 25 Tests from 1930 to 1947/48, he toured abroad three times, including the infamous 1932/33 Ashes series when he refused to adopt 'bodyline' tactics. He scored 750 runs with a top score of 122 versus New Zealand at Lord's in 1931 and he took 81 wickets with a best of 7 for 80 versus India at the Oval in 1936. He was the second oldest Test captain at 45 years 254 days, after W.G. Grace, when he led the MCC tour to the West Indies in 1947/48. He played 265 first-class matches scoring 9,232 runs and took 788 wickets. President of the MCC in 1963–4, the former 'Q' Stand at Lord's was named after him. He was knighted for his services to cricket in 1986 and died in 1989.

The 1921 Championship winning team. Back row, left to right: R.H. Twining, H.L. Dales, J.W. Hearne, F.J. Durston, A.R. Tanner, H.W. Lee. Front row: E.H. Hendren, N.E. Haig, F.T. Mann (captain), Hon. C.N. Bruce, H.R. Murrell.

The 1922 team. Back row, left to right: H.W. Lee, J.W. Hearne, G.E.V. Crutchley, F.J. Durston, G.T.S. Stevens, C.H. Gunasekera. Front row: E.H. Hendren, N.E. Haig, F.T. Mann (captain), Hon. C.N. Bruce, E.L. Kidd, H.R. Murrell.

The 1923 team. Back row, left to right: H.W. Lee, E. Martin, F.J. Durston, H.J. Wenyon, R.H. Hill. Front row: J.W. Hearne, N.E. Haig, E.H. Hendren, F.T. Mann (captain), H.R. Murrell, Hon. C.N. Bruce.

Henry Enthoven (1925-36). Born in Cartagena, Spain, in 1903, Henry Enthoven, was a right-handed middle-order batsman and a right-arm medium pace bowler. Schooled at Harrow, he went on to Cambridge University where he attained blues in all four years between 1923 and 1926. He made his Middlesex debut in 1925 and represented the county 123 times until 1936. For Middlesex he amassed 4,478 runs (av. 26.03) with 6 centuries and with a top score of 139. His best season was 1926 when he hit 1,129 runs (av. 31.36). He also took 100 wickets (av. 39.27) with a best performance of 5 for 29 and held 52 catches. He captained Cambridge in 1926 and Middlesex jointly with Nigel Haig between 1933 and 1934. He toured with the MCC to Canada in 1937 and his final first-class match was for the MCC in 1948. He died at Kensington in 1975.

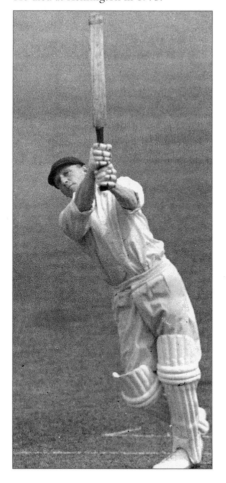

Walter Robins (1925–50). Born in Stafford in 1906, R.W.V. 'Walter' Robins was an outstanding right-handed all-rounder. He first appeared for Middlesex 1925 during his final term at Highgate School before going to Cambridge University, where he achieved a blue in each of his three years between 1926 and 1928. A dynamic captain who made things happen, he led Middlesex in three spells (1935 to 1938, 1946 to 1947 and 1950), winning the championship in 1947. For the county he played 258 matches scoring 9,337 runs (av. 26.37) with 6 centuries and a top score of 140. He took 669 wickets (av. 22.28) with a best performance of 8 for 69 versus Gloucestershire at Lord's in 1929 and held 142 catches. During his career he played 379 first-class matches, scoring 13,884 runs with 11 centuries, and recorded a top score of 140 versus Cambridge University at Fenner's in 1930. He took 969 wickets and held 221 catches. Representing England in 19 Tests between 1929 and 1937 he captained his country three times in 1937 versus New Zealand. He achieved 612 runs with a top score of 108 versus South Africa at Old Trafford in 1935 and bagged 64 wickets. He later acted as a Test selector (1946 to 1949, 1954 and 1964). He attained a blue at football while at Cambridge University and played for Nottingham Forest. He died at Marylebone, London, in 1968.

The 1926 team. Back row, left to right: R.H. Twining, H.L. Dales, J.W. Hearne, F.J. Durston, A.R. Tanner, H.W. Lee. Front row: E.H. Hendren, N.E. Haig, F.T. Mann (captain), Hon. C.N. Bruce, H.R. Murrell.

Fred Price (1926–47). A sound right-handed middle-order batsman and wicket-keeper, Fred Price was born in Westminster, London, in 1902. He represented Middlesex 382 times between 1926 and 1947. He accumulated 8,300 runs (av. 18.08) with three centuries, with a top score of 111, and held 627 catches and took 311 stumpings. He hit 1,000 runs in a season once, 1,298 (av. 25.96) in 1934. He played one Test for England in 1938 against Australia when he scored just 6 runs and took 2 catches. He toured twice with the MCC to the West Indies in 1929/30 and with Brinckman to Argentina in 1937/38. Between 1949 and 1967 he stood as a first-class umpire and caused a sensation by no-balling Tony Lock for throwing. He umpired 8 Tests between 1964 and 1967. He died at Hendon, Middlesex, in 1969.

The 1927 team. Back row, left to right: H.W. Lee, H.L. Dales, F.J. Durston, A.R. Tanner, J.W. Hearne. Middle row: E.H. Hendren, R.H. Twining, F.T. Mann (captain), G.E.V. Crutchley, H.R. Murrell. Front: G.T.S. Stevens.

Ian Peebles (1928–48). Ian was born in Aberdeen in 1908 where he was discovered at thirteen years of age by George Geary, after which he came south to play for Chiswick Park CC in London. Making his first-class debut at nineteen for the Gentlemen versus Players at the Oval in 1927, his first wicket was Andy Sandham. He later represented Middlesex from 1928 to 1948, playing 165 matches, he took 610 wickets (av. 19.87) with a best of 8 for 24 versus Worcestershire at Worcester in 1930, scored 1,361 runs (av. 8.95) with a top score of 58 and held 120 catches. Playing 251 first-class matches, during his career he took 923 wickets with a best performance of 8 for 24 versus Worcestershire at Worcester in 1930, and he scored 2,313 runs. He played only one Varsity match for Oxford University in 1930, taking 13 for 237 and also represented Scotland in 1937. Playing 13 Tests for England between 1927/28 and 1931 he toured overseas twice to South Africa. He took 45 Test wickets with a best performance of 6 for 63 versus South Africa at Johannesburg in 1930/31. Captaining Middlesex in 1939, his career ended tragically following damage to his eye in a wartime air raid. He subsequently entered the wine trade and later became the Cricket Correspondent of *The Times* and wrote several cricket books. He died at Speen, Buckinghamshire, in 1980.

The 1928 team. Back row, left to right: H.W. Lee, A.P. Powell, J.B. Wheatley, F.J. Durston, G.E. Hart, W.F.F. Price. Front row: R.H. Hill, J.W. Hearne, N.E. Haig (captain), E.H. Hendren, R.H.B. Bettington.

The 1929 team. Back row, left to right: H.W. Lee, H.J. Enthoven, G.C. Newman, F.J. Durston, W.F.F. Price, G.E. Hart, R.W.V. Robins. Front row: G.O.B. Allen, J.W. Hearne, N.E. Haig (captain), E.H. Hendren, Hon. C.N. Bruce.

George Newman (1929–36). Born in Paddington, London, in 1904, George Newman was a right-handed middle-order batsman and right-arm medium pace bowler. He attended Eton before going on to Oxford University where he attained blues in 1926 and 1927. He represented Middlesex fifty times between 1929 and 1936 and toured with the MCC to Canada in 1937. For Middlesex he scored 1,780 runs (av. 24.38) with 3 centuries including a top score of 112, took 10 wickets (av. 29.90) with a best of 4 for 18 and held 20 catches. During his career he accumulated 2,742 runs (av. 25.86) with three centuries and a top score of 112. He bagged 17 wickets (av. 39.41) with a best of 3 for 48 and held 27 catches. A noted athlete, he represented Oxford University in the high jump, the relay race, hurdles and squash, achieving a blue in the latter. He was President of Middlesex between 1963 and 1976. He died at Braintree, Essex, in 1982.

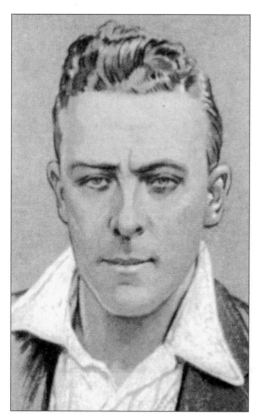

Joe Hulme (1929–39). Born in Stafford in 1904, Joe Hulme was a right-handed middle-order batsman, right-arm medium bowler and superb deep fieldsman. He represented Middlesex 223 times between 1929 and 1939, accumulating 8,015 runs (av. 26.62) with 12 centuries and a top score of 143. He hit 1,000 runs in a season three times with a best of 1,258 (av. 34.94) in 1934. He bagged 89 wickets (av. 36.21) with a best of 4 for 44 and held 109 catches. A well-respected footballer, he appeared at outside right for Blackburn Rovers, Arsenal and Huddersfield Town. He also played nine internationals for England between 1927 and 1929, scoring four goals. He died at Winchmore Hill, Middlesex, in 1991.

Jim Sims (1929–52). Born in Leyton, Essex, in 1903, Jim Sims was an attacking right-handed middle-order batsman and leg-break bowler. He represented Middlesex 381 times between 1929 and 1952 during which time he amassed 7,173 runs (av. 17.12) including three centuries, with a top score of 121 versus Northamptonshire at Kettering in 1937. He took 1,257 wickets (av. 25.22) with a best performance of 9 for 92 versus Lancashire at Old Trafford in 1934, and held 202 catches. He took 100 wickets in a season eight times with a best of 159 (av. 20.30) in 1939. He played 4 Tests for England between 1935 and 1936/37 taking 11 wickets (av. 43.63) with a best performance of 5 for 73; he scored 16 runs (av. 4.00) and held 4 catches. He toured overseas on three occasions, with the MCC to Australia and New Zealand in 1935/36 and 1936/37 and with Brinckman to South America in 1937/38. His best bowling performance was 10 for 90 for East versus West at Kingston-upon-Thames in 1948. His last first-class match was for the MCC in 1953. He became Middlesex coach between 1958 and 1960 and scorer between 1960 and 1972. He died at Canterbury, Kent, in 1973.

CHAPTER FOUR

THE THIRTIES

The 1930 team. Back row, left to right: H.W. Lee, H.J. Enthoven, G.C. Newman, E.G. Canning, W.F.F. Price, R.W.V. Robins. Front row: G.T.S. Stevens, J.W. Hearne, N.E. Haig (captain), E.H. Hendren, G.O.B. Allen.

The 1931 team. Back row, left to right: H.W. Lee, W.F.F. Price, I.A.R. Peebles, F.J. Durston, E.T. Killick, A.P. Powell. Front row: J.W. Hearne, N.E. Haig, F.T. Mann (captain), G.O.B. Allen, E.H. Hendren.

The 1932 team. Back row, left to right: H.W. Lee, F.J. Durston, G. E. Hart, W.F.F. Price, G. C. Newman, J.H.A. Hulme. Front row: I.A.R. Peebles, H.J. Enthoven, E.H. Hendren, G.T.S. Stevens, R. Beveridge.

Jack Young (1933–56). Born in Paddington, London, in 1912, Jack Young was a slow left-arm bowler, right-handed lower-order batsman and a fine gully fieldsman. Representing Middlesex 292 times between 1933 and 1956, he bagged 1,182 wickets (av. 19.21) with a best performance of 9 for 52 versus Gloucestershire at Cheltenham College in 1947. He scored 2,124 runs (av. 8.56) with a top score of 62 versus Yorkshire in 1949 and held 125 catches. He took 100 wickets in a season eight times with a best of 163 (av. 19.88) in 1952. He played 8 Tests for England between 1947 and 1949, and toured once with the MCC to South Africa in 1948/49. He took 17 wickets (av. 44.52) with a best haul of 3 for 65, scored 28 runs (av. 5.60) and held 5 catches. His best bowling performance in first-class cricket was 9 for 55 for an England XI versus a Commonwealth XI at Hastings in 1951. He died in London in 1993.

Len Muncer (1933–46). Born in Hampstead, London, in 1913, Len Muncer was a right-handed aggressive middle-order batsman and leg break and googly bowler, though he changed to off breaks during the 1947 season. Muncer was also a good slip fieldsman. He represented Middlesex eighty-two times between 1933 and 1946 before moving down to Wales. For Middlesex he scored 1,944 runs (av. 17.67), took 23 wickets (av. 28.17) and held 24 catches. He played 224 games for Glamorgan between 1947 and 1957 and was a member of their 1948 championship winning team. During his career he amassed 8,646 runs (av. 20.88) with four centuries and a top score of 135. He hit 1,000 runs in a season once in 1952 when he scored 1,097 (av. 24.37). He bagged 755 wickets (av. 20.90) with a best of 9 for 62 for Glamorgan versus Essex at Brentwood in 1948. He took 100 wickets in a season five times with a best of 159 (av. 17.27) in 1948. His last first-class match was for the MCC in 1957. After retiring from first-class cricket he became Head Coach at Lord's and ran a sports shop close to Lord's Cricket Ground. He died at Camden Town, London, in 1982.

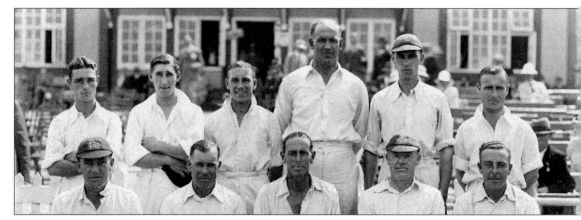

The 1933 team. Back row, left to right: J.A. Young, F.W. Punter, W.R. Watkins, F.J. Durston, J.M. Sims, P.G. Edwards. Front row: W.F.F. Price, E.H. Hendren, N.E. Haig (captain), J.M. Sims, J.H.A. Hulme.

Jim Smith (1934–9). Born in Corsham, Wiltshire, in 1906, brother of W.A. (Minor Counties), 'Big Jim' Smith was a right-arm fast bowler and right-handed lower-order batsman noted for his prowess as a six hitter. He represented Wiltshire in the minor county championship between 1926 and 1933 and made his first-class debut for Minor Counties in 1930. He joined Middlesex in 1934 and represented the county 152 times until his retirement in 1939. He bagged 676 wickets (av. 17.75) with a best performance of 8 for 102, took 5 wickets in an innings 39 times, scored 2,977 runs (av. 15.42) with a single century of 101 not out versus Kent at Canterbury in 1939 and held 69 catches. He took 100 wickets in a season four times with a best of 172 (av. 18.88) in 1934. He played 5 Tests for England between 1934/35 and 1937 and toured once to the West Indies in 1934/35. He took 15 wickets (av. 26.20) with a best haul of 5 for 26, scored 102 runs (av. 10.20) with a top score of 27 and held a single catch. Jim will be remembered for some remarkable hitting at Lord's: a shot through the committee room window; a huge hit over Father Time and a one-handed hit on to the pavilion roof, over the Tavern and across St John's Wood Road into the adjacent synagogue off the bowling of Yorkshire's George Macauley. He died at Mellor, near Blackburn, in 1979.

Laurie Gray (1934–51). Born in Tottenham in 1915, Laurie Gray was a right-arm fast-medium bowler and right-handed lower-order batsman. He represented the county 204 times between 1934 and 1951. He collected 600 wickets (av. 24.14) with a best performance of 8 for 59, and took 5 wickets in an innings 26 times. He scored 772 runs (av. 6.77) with a best score of 32 and held 119 catches. He later became a first-class umpire and stood between 1953 and 1970, officiating in two Test Matches between 1955 and 1963. He died at Langdon Hills, Essex, in 1983.

Dr Harold Owen-Smith (1935–7). Born in Rondebosch, Cape Town, South Africa, in 1909, Harold Owen-Smith was a useful right-handed middle-order batsman, slow leg-break bowler and excellent outfielder. Representing his native Western Province between 1927/28 and 1949/50 and Oxford University where he attained blues in all three years between 1931 and 1933, he represented Middlesex 28 times between 1935 and 1937. He scored 993 runs (av. 24.83) with a highest score of 77 and took 100 wickets (av. 21.50) with a best performance of 6 for 68 for the county, having held 27 catches. During his career he played 101 matches, accumulated 4,059 runs (av. 26.88) with three centuries and a top score of 168 not out, bagged 319 wickets (av. 23.22) with a best of 7 for 153 and held 93 catches. Playing 5 Tests for South Africa, he scored 252 runs (av. 42.00) with a top score of 129 and held 4 catches. He toured once to England in 1929, when he scored 1,168 runs (av. 35.89) and took 30 wickets (av. 25.80). A good all-round sportsman, he was awarded blues for boxing and rugby while at Oxford and went on to captain England at the former. He died at Rosebank, Cape Town, in 1990.

Denis Compton CBE (1936–58). Born in Hendon in 1918, Denis Compton, the 'Brylcreem Boy', was an outstanding sportsman. During the winter months he represented Arsenal (1935 to 1949) at football where he gained a wartime international cap, a league championship and FA Cup winners' medals. For Middlesex he amassed 21,781 runs (av. 49.95) with 67 centuries and 104 half-centuries, with a highest innings of 252 not out versus Somerset at Lord's in 1948. He bagged 477 wickets (av. 29.61), recording 5 wickets in an innings 16 times and 10 wickets in a match twice. His best performance was 6 for 80 (12 for 174 in the match) versus Surrey at the Oval in 1947. He held 264 catches. Playing 515 first-class matches during his career, he acquired 38,942 runs (av. 51.85) with 123 centuries, and reached a top score of 300 for the MCC versus North-Eastern Transvaal at Benoni in 1948/49. He took 622 wickets with a best of 7 for 36 with his spinners and held 416 catches. Playing 78 Tests for England between 1937 and 1956/57 he accumulated 5,807 runs (av. 50.06) with 17 centuries. His top score was 278 versus Pakistan at Trent Bridge in 1954; he toured overseas eight times. He also played in India for Holkar and Europeans between 1944 and 1946. In 1947 he achieved a record 18 first-class centuries while scoring 3,816 runs in the season. His third wicket stand of 424 with Bill Edrich versus Somerset at Lord's in 1948 remains the county record for any wicket partnership. He died in hospital in Windsor on St George's Day, 1997.

William 'Bill' Edrich DFC (1937–58). Born in Norfolk in 1916, Bill Edrich was a fearless all-rounder who won the DFC as a daylight RAF bomber pilot during the Second World War and was one of four brothers from a cricketing family who went on to play first-class cricket. He represented Middlesex 389 times from 1937 to 1958 (1953 to 1957 as captain) and accumulated 25,738 runs (av. 43.40) with 62 centuries and 135 half-centuries, of which his top score was 267 not out versus Northamptonshire at Northampton in 1947. He took 328 wickets (av. 30.41) recording 5 wickets in an innings 10 times, with a best of 7 for 48 versus Worcestershire at Worcester in 1946; he held 382 catches and even took 1 stumping. During his career he played 571 first-class matches, scoring 36,965 runs with 86 centuries. He also achieved 479 wickets with a best performance of 7 for 48, having taken 529 catches. Playing 9 Tests for England between 1938 and 1954/55 and touring overseas five times, he scored 2,440 runs with a best of 219 versus South Africa at Durban in 1938/39. He scored eight double centuries for Middlesex. He exceeded 2,000 runs in a season 9 times and hit 3,589 runs including 12 centuries in 1947, an aggregate only exceeded by Denis Compton. He represented Norfolk at minor county level and also played football for Norwich City and Tottenham Hotspur before the war. He died at Chesham, Buckinghamshire, in 1986.

The 1937 team. Back row, left to right: W.J. Edrich, B.L. Muncer, J.M. Sims, C.I.J. Smith, L.H. Gray, D.C.S. Compton, J.H.A. Hulme. Front row: H.G.O. Owen-Smith, E.H. Hendren, R.W.V. Robins (captain), W.H. Webster, W.F.F. Price.

George Mann CBE, DSO, MC (1937–54). George Mann was born in Byfleet, Surrey, in 1917 and captained Eton before representing Cambridge University in 1938 and 1939. A powerful middle-order batsman particularly strong on the leg side, he once hit a straight six over the main football stand roof at Headingley on to the adjacent rugby field. Playing for Middlesex from 1937 to 1954, he played 54 matches for the county, scoring 3,403 runs (av. 24.65) with 3 centuries and a top score of 116. He took just 2 wickets (av. 22.50) with a best of 2 for 16 and held 41 catches. Playing 166 first-class matches, during his career he scored 6,350 runs with a career best 136 not out for England versus South Africa at Port Elizabeth in 1948/49. Captaining the county in 1948 and 1949, he was unable to lead the 1950/51 MCC tour to Australia because of commitments at his family-owned brewery, but still played 7 Tests between 1948 and 1949. The Mann family provided the only example of successive generations skippering England in a single Test. He later acted as TCCB Chairman from 1978 to 1983 following the 'Packer' affair and subsequently became President of the MCC in 1984/85.

Jack Robertson (1937–59). A stylish right-handed opening batsman, fine off-break bowler and good fieldsman, Jack Robertson was born in Chiswick in 1917. He represented Turnham Green CC where he opened the batting with his father. The ex-county professional Jack Durston coached him before he made his Middlesex debut in 1937. For the county he played 423 matches, scoring 27,088 runs (av. 38.96) with 59 centuries, including a ground record top score made in one day of 331 not out versus Worcestershire at New Road in 1949. He took 56 wickets (av. 35.82) with a best of 4 for 37 and held 301 catches. During his career he played 509 first-class matches until he retired in 1959, during which time he accumulated 31,914 runs with 67 centuries. He achieved 1,000 runs in a season fourteen times, his best season being 1951 when he amassed 2,917 runs. He also took 73 wickets and held 350 catches. For England he played 11 Tests scoring 881 runs with a top score of 133 versus the West Indies in Port of Spain in 1947/48; he toured overseas just twice. In 1948 at Lord's he scored 9 runs off a single delivery (4 coming from an overthrow) from H.S. Squires for the MCC versus Surrey. After retiring he acted as county coach. He died at Bury St Edmunds, Suffolk, in 1996.

Syd Brown (1937–55). Born in Eltham, Kent, in 1917, Syd Brown was a forceful right-handed opening batsman, a good deep fieldsman and occasional wicket-keeper. He represented Middlesex 313 times between 1937 and 1955 and made his debut for the county against Oxford University at the Parks in 1937 when his opening partner was fellow debutant E.W. 'Jim' Swanton. For the county he amassed 15,050 runs (av. 29.51) with 20 centuries and 78 half-centuries and achieved a top score of 232 not out versus Somerset at Lord's in 1951. He hit 1,000 runs in a season nine times, exceeding 2,000 runs in a season once, 2,078 runs (av. 37.78) in 1947. He also took 146 catches, 2 stumpings and 3 wickets (av. 26.66) with a best of 2 for 19. Syd Brown was one of the finest fieldsmen and could get down, pick the ball up and throw it in – all in one movement – while running in at full speed. He died in 1987.

The 1938 team. Back row, left to right: L. D'Arcy, L. Hart, L.B. Muncer, C.I.J. Smith, W.T. Nevell, L.H. Gray, D.C.S. Compton. Front row: W.F.F. Price, E.H. Hendren, H.J. Enthoven, W.H. Webster, J.H.A. Hulme. Insets: left R.W.V. Robins (captain), right G.O.B. Allen.

Leslie Compton (1938–56). Born in Woodford, Essex, in 1912, Leslie Compton, brother of course of Denis, was a right-handed lower-order batsman, wicket-keeper and right-arm medium-pace bowler. He represented Middlesex 272 times from 1938 to 1956 during which time he scored 5,781 runs (av. 16.85) with a single century of 107 versus Derbyshire at Derby in 1947. As a wicket-keeper he held 465 catches and took 131 stumpings and as an occasional bowler took 12 wickets (av. 47.42) with a best performance of 2 for 21. A noted football player, he was centre-half for Arsenal when they won the FA Cup in 1950 against Liverpool at Wembley (2-0) and in 1950/51 he gained two caps for England – against Wales at Roker Park, Sunderland (4-2), and against Yugoslavia at Highbury (2-2). Between 1931 and 1951 he played 253 matches for Arsenal, scoring 5 goals. He died at Hendon, Middlesex, in 1984.

CHAPTER FIVE

FORTIES & CHAMPIONS

The 1947 Championship winning team. Back row, left to right: P.I. Bedford, A.W. Thompson, L.H. Gray, L.H. Compton, J.D.B. Robertson, S.M. Brown, J.A. Young. Front row: W.J. Edrich, F.G. Mann, R.W.V. Robins (captain), J.M. Sims, D.C.S. Compton.

Middlesex County Cricket Club, 1948
(Champion County 1947)

[autograph signatures]

Champion County 1947 autograph sheet.

Ian Bedford (1947–62). Born in Friern Barnet, Middlesex, in 1930, Ian Bedford was a lower-order right-handed batsman and leg-break bowler. He made his Middlesex debut in 1947 aged seventeen. His first season was impressive – he finished second in the county bowling averages with 25 wickets (av. 19.36), but he failed to maintain that early form and decided to leave county cricket. In 1961 Middlesex recalled him as captain and he led the county for two seasons. For Middlesex he played 65 matches scoring 772 runs (av. 15.69), took 103 wickets 9 (av. 32.71) and held 34 catches. During his career he played 77 first-class matches scoring 979 runs (av. 16.31) with a top score of 75 not out versus Gloucestershire at Gloucester in 1961. He bagged 128 wickets (av. 32.87) with a best performance of 6 for 52 versus Yorkshire at Bradford in 1948 and held 46 catches. He toured overseas on three occasions to South America in 1958/59 and 1963/64 and North America in 1959. Sadly he collapsed while batting in a club match at Buckhurst Hill CC, Essex, in 1966 and died on the way to Wanstead Hospital.

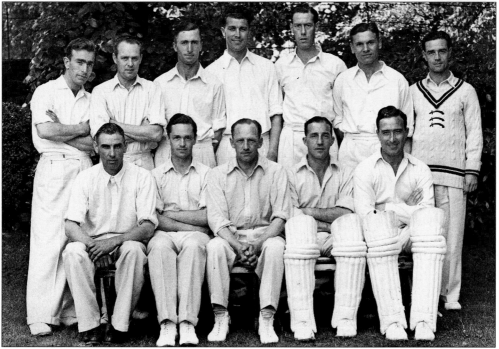

The 1948 team. Back row, left to right: J.T. Eaglestone, A.W. Thompson, J.D.B. Robertson, L.H. Compton, L.H. Gray, S.M. Brown, J.A. Young. Front row: J.M. Sims, F.G. Mann, R.W.V. Robins (captain), W.J. Edrich, D.C.S. Compton.

John Dewes (1948–56). Born in North Latchford, Cheshire, in 1926, John Dewes was a left-handed opening batsman, right-arm medium-pace bowler and excellent outfielder. Schooled at Aldenham, he went on to Cambridge University where he attained blues all three years between 1948 and 1950. He represented Middlesex from 1948 to 1956 on 62 occasions, scoring 3,589 runs (av. 38.18) with 10 centuries; this included a top score of 139. He took 1 wicket for 10 (av. 10.00) and held 21 catches. His career best score was 212 for Cambridge University versus Sussex at Hove in 1950. He hit 1,000 runs in a season three times with a best of 2,432 runs (av. 59.31) in 1950. He represented England in 5 Tests between 1948 and 1950/51 scoring 121 runs (av. 12.10) with a top score of 67 versus the West Indies at Trent Bridge in 1950, and toured overseas once to Australia and New Zealand in 1950/51. His appearances for Middlesex were restricted during the 1950s by his profession as a teacher. He made his first-class debut at Lord's in 1945 for England versus Australia and his final appearance for L.E.G. Ames' XI in 1957. A good hockey player, he gained blues in 1949 and 1950. His son A.R. represented Cambridge University between 1978 and 1979, attaining a blue in 1978.

The 1949 joint Championship winning team. Back row, left to right: J.A. Young, S.M. Brown, L.H. Gray, J.J. Warr, L.H. Compton, H.P.H. Sharp. Middle row: J.D.B. Robertson, J.M. Sims, R.W.V. Robins (captain), W.J. Edrich, D.C.S. Compton. Front row: A.W. Thompson, J.G. Dewes.

CHAPTER SIX

FIFTIES & SIXTIES

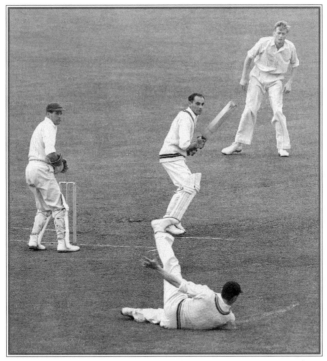

Harry Sharp (1946–55). Born in Kentish Town, London, in 1917, Harry Sharp was a sound right-handed opening batsman and off-break bowler. He represented the county in 162 matches between 1946 and 1955. He accumulated 6,141 runs (av. 25.80) with nine centuries and a highest innings of 165 not out versus Northamptonshire in 1951. He achieved 50 wickets (av. 32.56) with a best performance of 5 for 52 and held 59 catches. He hit 1,000 runs in a season on three occasions, with a best of 1,564 (av. 32.58) in 1953. His last first-class match was for the MCC in 1957. He was Middlesex's scorer between 1974 and 1993 when computerised scoring was introduced. He died close to his home in Enfield in 1995.

Fred Titmus MBE (1949–82). Born in Kentish Town, London, in 1932, a talented all-rounder, he made his Middlesex debut aged sixteen in 1949 as a right-arm off-spin bowler and right-handed batsman. For Middlesex he played 642 matches scoring 17,320 runs (av. 22.78) with 4 centuries and a top score of 120 not out versus Sussex at Hove in 1961. He took 2,361 wickets (av. 21.27) with a best of 9 for 52 versus Cambridge University at Fenner's in 1962. He took 5 wickets in an innings 146 times and 10 wickets in a match 20 times and held 378 catches. His career spanned five decades until 1982, during which time he played 792 first-class matches, scoring 21,558 runs; he took 2,830 wickets and held 473 catches. He achieved the double on eight occasions and bagged 100 wickets in a season sixteen times with a best of 191 in 1955. His career best performance with the bat was 137 not out for England versus South Australia at Adelaide in 1962/63. Playing 53 Tests between 1955 and 1974/75 he toured overseas nine times scoring 1,449 runs with a best of 84 not out versus India at Bombay in 1963/64, and he took 153 wickets with a best performance of 7 for 79 versus Australia at Sydney in 1962/63. He represented Orange Free State in 1975/76 and Surrey in 1978, where he later acted as coach. A Test selector from 1986 to 1988, he ran a sub-post office in Potten End, near Hemel Hempstead, for many years.

Don Bennett (1950–68). Born in Wakefield, Yorkshire, in 1933, Don Bennett had lived in Middlesex since 1940 and attended Ashford County Grammar School in order to gain his residential qualification for the county. A right-handed middle-order batsman and right-arm fast-medium bowler he represented the county on 392 occasions between 1950 and 1968. He accumulated 10,274 runs (av. 21.85) with 4 centuries and a top score of 117 not out versus Yorkshire at Headingley in 1964 when he added 220 for the seventh wicket with J.T. Murray. He scored 1,000 runs in a season twice with a best of 1,144. As a strike bowler, he bagged 748 wickets (av. 26.45) with a best performance of 7 for 47 versus Sussex at Hove in 1956, and held 156 catches. A noted footballer, he represented Arsenal and Coventry City in seventy-three matches without scoring a goal. After retiring he became an invaluable member of the Middlesex staff as county coach and was responsible for the 1st XI until his retirement in 1997. He is now a general member of the club committee.

The 1952 team. Back row, left to right: D.L. Newman, R. Routledge, J.A. Young, D. Bennett, H.P.H. Sharp, A. Fairbairn. Front row: S.M. Brown, J.M. Sims, W.J. Edrich, J.D.B. Robertson, L.H. Compton.

John Murray MBE (1952–75). Born in North Kensington, London, in 1935, wicket-keeper and batsman, John 'JT' Murray represented Middlesex from 1952 to 1975. He played 508 matches for the county, scoring 15,251 runs (av. 23.24) with 11 centuries with a top score of 133 not out versus Oxford University at the Parks in 1963. He held 1,024 catches, took 199 stumpings and 4 wickets (av. 33.50) with a best of 1 for 1. Playing 635 first-class matches during his career, he scored 18,872 runs with a top score of 142 and took 6 wickets with his right-arm medium-pacers. He established a world record of 1,527 dismissals (1,270 catches and 257 stumpings) during his career, until surpassed by Bob Taylor in 1982/83. He achieved the record of scoring 1,000 runs and taking 100 dismissals in a season in 1957, the only player to do so since Les Ames in 1932. Making twenty-one Test appearances for England between 1961 and 1967, he scored 506 runs with a top score of 112 versus the West Indies at the Oval in 1966, when he added 217 runs for the eighth wicket with Tom Graveney. He achieved 55 Test dismissals and toured overseas eleven times. He holds the record for the most dismissals in a career by a Middlesex player – 1,223 – and for the most in a match – 9 – versus Hampshire at Lord's in 1965. In 1977/78 he acted as an England Test selector.

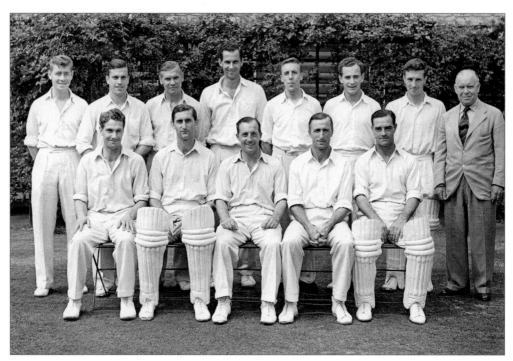

The 1954 team. Back row, left to right: R.V. Bell, D. Bennett, S.M. Brown, A.E. Moss, J.T. Murray, G.P.S. Delisle, F.J. Titmus, E.H. Hendren (scorer). Front row: J.G. Dewes, J.J. Warr, W.J. Edrich (captain), J.D.B. Robertson, J.A. Young.

Donald Bick (1954–67). Born in Hampstead, London, in 1936, Don Bick was a useful right-handed batsman and right-arm off-spin bowler. He represented the county in 145 matches between 1954 and 1967 scoring 2,136 runs (av. 13.51), with a top score of 67 versus Cambridge University at Fenner's in 1957. He bagged 229 wickets (av. 27.63) with joint best performances of 5 for 22 versus Yorkshire at Scarborough in 1959 and versus Cambridge University at Fenner's in 1965, and held 35 catches. After retiring from first-class cricket he represented Hertfordshire in the minor county championship.

The 1955 team. Back row, left to right: R.J. Hurst, D. Bennett, H.P.H. Sharp, D.O. Baldry, A.E. Moss, F.J. Titmus. Front row: J.D.B. Robertson, D.C.S. Compton, W.J. Edrich (captain), J.J. Warr, L.H. Compton, J.A. Young.

The 1956 team. Back row, left to right: R.V. Bell, J.A. Young, S.M. Brown, A.E. Moss, D. Bennett D.O. Baldry, F.J. Titmus. Front row: J.D.B. Robertson, D.C.S. Compton, W.J. Edrich, J.J. Warr, L.H. Compton.

Peter Parfitt (1956–72). Born in Billingford in 1936, Peter Parfitt joined Middlesex after representing his native Norfolk at minor county level. As a left-handed batsman, right-arm off-break bowler and fine fielder, he captained the county from 1968 to 1970 and retired in 1972. He represented the county 387 times, scoring 21,304 runs (av. 36.66) with 46 centuries and 114 half-centuries with a top score of 200 not out versus Nottinghamshire at Trent Bridge in 1964. He bagged 231 wickets (av. 27.80) with a best of 6 for 45 versus Oxford University at the Parks in 1969; he held 452 catches. Playing 498 first-class matches during his career, he scored 26,924 runs with 58 centuries and recorded a top score of 200 not out. He took 277 wickets with a best performance of 6 for 45 versus Oxford University at the Parks in 1969 and held 564 catches. He holds the county record for the most catches held in a season by a non-wicket-keeper – 46 in 1960 and 1966. Representing England in 37 Tests between 1961/62 and 1972, he toured overseas eight times, scored 1,882 runs with seven centuries including a top score of 131 not out versus New Zealand at Auckland in 1962/63. His best series was against Pakistan in 1962 when he amassed 340 runs with three centuries. Since retiring he has owned a pub and is now involved in corporate hospitality at major sporting events.

The 1958 team. Back row, left to right: D.E. Montague (physiotherapist), D. Bennett, D.A. Bick, H.W. Tilly, R.A. Gale, W.E. Russell, J.T. Murray, P.H. Parfitt, D.O. Baldry, E.H. Hendren (scorer). Front row: A.C. Walton, J.D.B. Robertson, J. Warr (captain), A.E. Moss, F.J. Titmus.

John Warr (1949–60). Born in Ealing in 1927, John 'JJ' Warr was a right-arm fast-medium bowler and right-handed tail-end batsman. He won blues all four years between 1949 and 1952 while at Cambridge University and captained the side in 1951. 'JJ' represented Middlesex 260 times between 1949 and 1960 taking 703 wickets (av. 20.75), with a best performance of 9 for 65 (14 for 92 in the match) versus Kent at Lord's in 1956. He scored 2,744 runs (av. 10.80) with a highest score of 53 versus Gloucestershire at Bristol in 1952 and held 91 catches. Captaining the county between 1958 and 1960, he exceeded 100 wickets in a season twice with a best of 116 (av. 18.17) in 1956. He played 2 Tests for England with a best of 1 for 76, his only wicket being that of Australian Ian Johnson, caught behind by Godfrey Evans. He toured overseas five times with the MCC to Australia and New Zealand in 1950/51, Canada in 1951, East Africa in 1957/58, E.W. Swanton's XI to the West Indies in 1955/56 and the Duke of Norfolk's XI to Jamaica in 1956/57. In 1991 he was elected a Trustee of the MCC and in 1987/88 he served as President of the club. Retiring from first-class cricket in 1960, he concentrated on a career in the City and is a member of the Jockey Club, a senior steward at Goodwood and a highly respected and amusing after-dinner speaker.

Alan Moss (1950–63). Born in Tottenham in 1930, Alan Moss was a right-arm fast-medium bowler and right-handed tail-end batsman. He represented Middlesex 307 times between 1950 and 1963, during which time he bagged 1,088 wickets (av. 19.81) with a best performance of 8 for 31 versus Northamptonshire at Kettering in 1960. A stubborn batsman, he accumulated 1,234 runs (av. 6.56) with a top score of 40 versus Surrey at the Oval in 1962 and held 121 catches. He took 100 wickets in a season five times with a best haul of 136 (av. 13.72) in 1960. Halfway through the 1962 season he took over the captaincy from Ian Bedford and did an excellent job. He was a very popular figure with his fellow players and was well-respected as captain. He represented England in 9 Tests between 1953/54 and 1960 taking 21 wickets (av. 29.80) with a best performance of 4 for 35; he scored 61 runs (av. 10.16) with a top score of 26 and held a single catch. On his retirement at the age of thirty-three he ran a printing business, and is presently chairman of the county club.

Dennis Baldry (1953–8). Born in Acton, London, in 1931, Dennis Baldry was a right-handed middle-order batsman and a useful off-break bowler. He played 49 first-class matches for the county, accumulating 1,155 runs (av. 14.62) with a top score of 61 versus Worcestershire at Kidderminster in 1957. He took 11 wickets (av. 31.09) with a best performance of 4 for 60 and held 22 catches. After six seasons with Middlesex he moved to Hampshire for whom he played 85 matches between 1959 and 1962. He hit 151 for Hampshire on his debut versus Glamorgan at Portsmouth in 1959.

Bob Gale (1956–65). Born in Old Warden, Bedfordshire, in 1933, Bob Gale was a left-handed opening batsman and right-arm medium-pace or leg-break bowler. Schooled at Bedford Modern, he made his first-class debut for the Army in 1955 before representing Middlesex 219 times between 1956 and 1965. He amassed 11,234 runs (av. 29.10) with 13 centuries and a top score of 200 versus Glamorgan at Rodney Parade, Newport, in 1962. He hit 1,000 runs in a season six times with a best of 2,211 (av. 38.78) in 1962. He achieved 46 wickets (av. 33.15) with a best performance of 4 for 57, and held 108 catches. He toured overseas three times with E.W. Swanton to the West Indies in 1960/61, F.R. Brown to East Africa in 1961/62 and the MCC to South America in 1964/65. His final first-class match was for the Free Foresters in 1968. Elected to the general committee in 1989, he served as chairman of the cricket sub-committee until 1998.

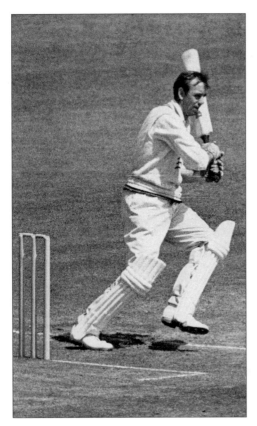

Eric Russell (1956–72). Born in Dumbarton in 1936, Russell joined Middlesex in 1956 as a right-handed opening batsman and right-arm medium-pace bowler. For Middlesex he scored 23,103 runs (av. 35.11) with 11 centuries; his top score was 193 versus Hampshire at Bournemouth in 1964. He took 10 wickets (av. 64.30) with a best of 2 for 46 and held 274 catches. During his career he played 448 first-class matches; he accumulated 25,525 runs (av. 34.87) with 41 centuries, of which his 193 at Bournemouth was his best. He took 22 wickets with a best performance of 3 for 20 and held 304 catches. He hit 1,000 runs in a season thirteen times, going on to 2,000 runs in a season three times with a best of 2,343 (av. 45.92) in 1964. Playing in 10 Tests for England between 1961/62 and 1967 against six different Test nations, he scored 362 runs with a top score of 70 versus South Africa at the Oval in 1965; he held 4 catches and toured overseas three times. After retiring in 1972 he taught at Shiplake College and in recent years he has been involved at the MCC's Shenley Cricket Centre in Hertfordshire which was renamed the Denis Compton Ground in 1995. Eric has been a member of the club committee since 1996 and is a life member of the Hertfordshire Cricket Society, having served as Chairman from 1995 to 1998.

Ron Hooker (1956–69). Born in Lower Clapton, London, in 1935, Ron Hooker was a right-arm medium-pace bowler and right-handed middle-order batsman. He represented the county in 300 matches and amassed 8,222 runs (av. 22.16) with 5 centuries and a top score of 137 versus Kent at Gravesend in 1959. He bagged 490 wickets (av. 27.46) with a best performance of 7 for 18 versus Worcestershire at Worcester in 1965, and held 301 catches. He hit 1,000 runs in a season twice with a best of 1,449 (av. 30.18) in 1959. He scored an 87 minute century in 1966 against Somerset at Weston-super-Mare. When he came to the wicket with Middlesex on 110 for 5, he hit 102 out of 120 and thanks to this the county went on to win the match easily. In one of his last performances for Middlesex in the John Player Sunday League he took 6 wickets for just 6 runs as Surrey were dismissed for only 83.

Bob White (1958–65). Born in Fulham, London, in 1936, Bob 'Knocker' White was a sound left-handed opening or middle-order batsman and off-break bowler. He represented Middlesex 114 times between 1958 and 1965 before moving to Trent Bridge in 1966. He played 114 matches for the county, scoring 4,140 runs (av. 24.79) with a top score of 108 not out versus Northamptonshire at Peterborough in 1963, and held 50 catches. He made 298 appearances for Nottinghamshire between 1966 and 1980. His best season with the bat was 1963 when he recorded 1,355 runs (av. 33.87), and with the ball 1971, when he took 81 wickets (av. 26.21). During his career he amassed 12,452 runs (av. 23.18) with 5 centuries of which his highest score was 116 not out for Nottinghamshire versus Surrey at the Oval in 1967. He took 693 wickets (av. 30.50) with a best haul of 7 for 41 for Nottinghamshire versus Derbyshire at Ilkeston in 1971, and held 190 catches. His career was quite remarkable in that he did not take any wickets at all during his eight seasons at Middlesex. In 1983 he was elected to the first-class umpires list.

Ted Clark (1959–76). Born in Balham, South London, in 1937, Ted Clark was a right-handed middle-order batsman and left-arm medium-pace bowler. He represented the county 196 times from 1959 to 1976. He amassed 8,595 runs (av. 29.33) with 6 centuries and a top score of 149 versus Kent at Gravesend in 1966. He took 58 wickets (av. 32.41) with a best performance of 5 for 61 versus Surrey at the Oval in 1964 and held 105 catches. He achieved 1,000 runs in a season five times with a best of 1,454 runs (av. 32.31) in 1964. He toured four times with the MCC to East Africa in 1973/74, West Africa in 1975/76 and Bangladesh in 1976/77 and 1978/79. He ceased to appear regularly for the county after 1966. Since retiring he has served as a member of the general club committee.

Mike Smith (1959–80). Born in Enfield, Middlesex, in 1942, and schooled at Enfield Grammar, Mike Smith was a sound right-handed opening batsman and slow left-arm bowler. He represented Middlesex 399 times between 1959 and 1980 while accumulating 18,575 runs (av. 31.64) with 37 centuries including a highest score of 181 versus Lancashire at Old Trafford in 1967. He took 57 wickets (av. 32.57) with a best performance of 4 for 13 versus Gloucestershire at Lord's in 1961 and held 210 catches. He hit 1,000 runs in a season eleven times with a best of 1,705 (av. 39.65) in 1970. He toured overseas four times with Derrick Robins' XI to South Africa in 1972/73 and 1973/74, the West Indies in 1974/75 and Sri Lanka in 1977/78. He played for England in one-day Internationals against the West Indies in 1976. Since 1994 he has been the county's scorer, taking over from Harry Sharp.

The 1962 team. Back row, left to right: P.H. Parfitt, W.E. Russell, C.D. Drybrough, M.J. Smith, R.A. Gale, E.A. Clark, R.W. Hooker. Front row: J.T. Murray, A.E. Moss, P.I. Bedford (captain), F.J. Titmus, D. Bennett.

The 1964 team. Back row, left to right: J.M. Sims (scorer), J.M. Brearley, M.J. Smith, J.S.E. Price, E.A. Clark, R.W. Hooker, R.A. White, R.I.A. Nicholas (masseur). Front row: J.T. Murray, P.H. Parfitt, D. Bennett, C.D. Drybrough (captain), F.J. Titmus, W.E. Russell.

MIDDLESEX COUNTY CRICKET CLUB

Centenary Dinner

in The Great Room, Grosvenor House,*
Park Lane, London w 1
on Monday, 20th July, 1964
7.15 p.m. for 7.45 p.m. **Lounge Suit**

*Park Lane Entrance

To gain admission, please bring this ticket with you

Ticket for Middlesex County Cricket Club centenary dinner in 1964.

Michael Harris (1964–8). Born in St Just-in-Roseland, Cornwall, in 1944, Mike 'Pasty' Harris was a right-handed opening batsman, leg-break bowler and wicket-keeper. He represented Middlesex 72 times between 1964 and 1968 scoring 3,371 runs (av. 31.50) with 6 centuries and with a top score of 160 versus Pakistan at Lord's in 1967, when he shared a first wicket partnership of 312 with Eric Russell. He took 2 wickets (av. 42.50) with a best of 1 for 4 and held 27 catches. He moved to Nottinghamshire, whom he represented in 261 matches between 1969 and 1982. He spent two winters abroad with Eastern Province in 1971/72 and Wellington in 1975/76 and toured the West Indies in 1974/75 with Derrick Robins' XI. During his career he amassed 19,196 runs (av. 36.70) with 41 centuries and a top score of 201 not out for Nottinghamshire versus Glamorgan at Trent Bridge in 1973. He hit 1,000 runs in a season eleven times, achieving 2,000 once. His best season was 1971, with 2,238 (av. 50.86). He bagged 79 wickets (av. 43.78) with a best of 4 for 16 versus Warwickshire at Trent Bridge in 1969; he held 288 catches and took 14 stumpings. He later became a first-class umpire.

Clive Radley (1964–87). A right-handed middle-order batsman, leg-break bowler and good close fielder, he was born in Hertford in 1944, and made his county debut against Lancashire in 1964. He represented Middlesex in 520 matches between 1964 and 1987 amassing 24,147 runs (av. 35.45) with 42 centuries and a top score of 200 in 1985. He took 8 wickets (av. 19.50) with a best of 2 for 38 and held 486 catches. He hit 1,000 runs in a season sixteen times with a best of 1,491 (av. 57.34) in 1980. Radley played 8 Tests for England scoring 481 runs (av. 48.10) with a top score of 158 versus New Zealand in 1977/78. He toured overseas five times with Derrick Robins to South Africa in 1972/73 and 1974/75, England to Pakistan and New Zealand in 1977/78, Australia in 1978/79 and Middlesex to Zimbabwe in 1980/81, and wintered with Auckland in 1984/85. Against the touring South Africans at Lord's, Radley shared a sixth wicket stand of 277 with Fred Titmus. A prolific scorer in limited overs matches, he is remembered for his 133 against Glamorgan in the John Player Sunday League in 1969. His 85 not out against Glamorgan in the Gillette Cup Final 1977, 89 not out against Essex in the Benson & Hedges Cup Final 1983, and 67 against Kent in the NatWest Trophy Final 1984 epitomise his reliability. Since retiring he has captained the 2nd XI and is now MCC's Head Coach at Lord's.

The 1965 team. Back row, left to right: R.S. Herman, C.T. Radley, E.A. Clark, R.W. Hooker, J.S.E. Price, D.A. Bick, P.H. Parfitt. Front row: R.A. Gale, D. Bennett, F.J. Titmus (captain), J.T. Murray, W.E. Russell.

Bob Herman (1965–71). Born in Shirley, Southampton, in 1946, the son of O.W. 'Lofty' (Hampshire), Bob Herman was a right-arm fast-medium bowler and right-handed lower-order batsman. He represented the county 92 times between 1965 and 1971 before joining Hampshire. For Middlesex he took 196 wickets (av. 29.35) with a best of 6 for 32 versus Oxford University at the Parks in 1969, scored 453 (av. 8.23) with a top score of 40 not out versus Surrey at the Oval in 1967 and held 37 catches. He played 89 matches for Hampshire between 1972 and 1977 and wintered overseas twice in South Africa, playing for Border in 1971/72 and Griqualand West in 1974/75. During his career he achieved 506 wickets (av. 26.37) with a best of 8 for 42 versus Warwickshire at Portsmouth in 1972, and scored 1,426 runs (av. 10.18) with a top score of 56 versus Worcestershire at Portsmouth in 1972, and held 74 catches. He later played for Dorset between 1978 and 1979 in the minor county championship and between 1980 and 1982 was a first-class umpire.

Harry Latchman (1965–73). Born in Kingston, Jamaica, in 1943, Amritt Harrichand known as 'Harry' Latchman was a lower-order right-handed batsman and leg-break and googly bowler. He represented Middlesex from 1965 to 1973 playing 170 first-class matches before moving on to Nottinghamshire between 1974 and 1976 where he played a further 40 first-class matches. For Middlesex he scored 1,950 runs (av. 14.55) with a top score of 96, bagged 400 wickets (av. 27.58) with a best of 7 for 91 versus Pakistan at Lord's in 1967; he recorded 5 wickets in an innings 18 times, and held 79 catches. During his career he played 210 first-class matches scoring 2,333 runs (av. 13.25) with a top score of 96 versus Worcestershire at Kidderminster in 1972, bagged 487 wickets (av. 27.90) with a best performance of 7 for 65 and held 107 catches. He toured once in 1967/68 with an International XI to Ceylon and India and has toured in more recent years with MCC teams to Italy, the USA and Japan. He played two seasons of minor county cricket for Cambridgeshire between 1977 and 1978. A regular visitor to Lord's, he is presently cricket coach at Merchant Taylors' School in Northwood, Middlesex.

The 1966 team. Back row, left to right: J.D.B. Robertson (coach), C.T. Radley, M.J. Smith, J.S.E. Price, M.J. Harris, R.S. Herman, H.C. Latchman. Front row: W.E. Russell, J.T. Murray, F.J. Titmus (captain), P.H. Parfitt, R.W. Hooker.

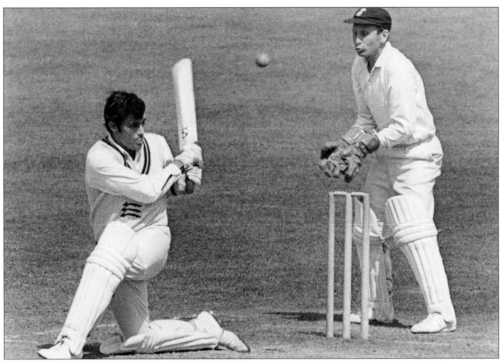

Ken Jones (1967–74). Born in Park Royal in 1942, Jones was a right-arm medium-pace bowler and right-handed batsman. He represented the county 117 times between 1967 and 1974. He scored 2,031 runs (av. 17.21) with a top score of 57 not out versus Surrey at the Oval in 1972 and bagged 241 wickets (av. 27.04) with a best performance of 7 for 52 versus Warwickshire at Coventry in 1971; he held 48 catches. He later played for Bedfordshire in the minor county championship.

The 1967 team. Back row, left to right: J.M. Sims (scorer), C.T. Radley, M.J. Harris, J.S.E. Price, R.S. Herman, M.J. Smith, H.C. Latchman, R.I.A. Nicholas (masseur). Front row: W.E. Russell, J.T. Murray, F.J. Titmus (captain), R.W. Hooker, P.H. Parfitt.

Alan Connolly (1969–70). Born in Skipton, Victoria, Australia, in 1939, Alan Connolly was a right-arm fast-medium bowler and right-handed lower-order batsman. He represented his native Victoria 83 times between 1959/60 and 1970/71 and Australia in 29 Tests between 1964/65 and 1970/71. He toured six times to England in 1964 and 1968, South Africa in 1969/70, India in 1964/65 and 1969/70 and New Zealand in 1966/67. He joined Middlesex in 1969 and played 44 times for the county until 1970/71 when he returned to Australia and retired with a back injury. For Middlesex he bagged 126 wickets (av. 26.42) with a best of 6 for 39 versus Lancashire at Lord's in 1970, scored 180 runs (av. 6.00) with a highest score of 26 and held 8 catches. During the 1969 season Connolly took 74 wickets (av. 23.24). His best bowling performance in first-class matches was 9 for 67 for Victoria versus Queensland at Brisbane in 1964/65.

CHAPTER SEVEN

BREARLEY'S CHAMPIONS

Mike Brearley (1961–83). Born in Harrow in 1942, Brearley was an excellent tactical captain who made his first-class debut for Cambridge University in 1961, and acted as captain in 1963 and 1964. He represented Middlesex 292 times from 1961 to 1983 (1971 to 1982 as captain), as an opening batsman and specialist slip fielder, leading the county to the championship three times and once shared. For the county he accumulated 15,985 runs (av. 38.33) with 29 centuries and 85 half-centuries. His highest innings was 173 not out versus Glamorgan at Cardiff in 1974. He took 1 wicket (av. 119.00) with a best of 1 for 6, held 211 catches and took 1 stumping. During his career he played 455 first-class matches, accumulating 25,185 runs with 45 centuries and a top score of 312 not out for the MCC Under 25 versus North Zone at Peshawar in 1966/67 and held 418 catches. He represented England in 39 Tests, with eighteen victories in 31 Tests as skipper, scoring 1,442 runs with a top score of 91 versus India at Bombay in 1976/77. He toured overseas ten times and was only the second captain after Len Hutton to regain and successfully defend the Ashes. Brearley was also the first to lead England to five wins in an Ashes series. Since his retirement he has concentrated on psychotherapy, cricket writing and teaching.

The 1971 team. Back row, left to right: K.V. Jones, C.J.R. Black, M.J. Smith, J.S.E. Price, T. Selwood, C.T. Radley, J.D. Hopkins. Middle row: P.H. Parfitt, F.J. Titmus, J.M. Brearley (captain), J.T. Murray, W.E. Russell. Front row: N.G. Featherstone, H.C. Latchman.

John Price (1961–75). Born in Harrow in 1937, John Price was a right-arm fast-medium bowler and lower-order left-handed batsman. Making his county debut in 1961 for Middlesex he played 242 matches until 1975, taking 734 wickets (av. 22.39) with a best performance of 8 for 48 versus Derbyshire at Lord's in 1966. He recorded 5 wickets in an innings 25 times and 10 wickets in a match 4 times. He scored 902 runs (av. 8.20) with a top score of 41 not out and held 89 catches. His best season was 1966 when he bagged 94 wickets (av. 18.74). During his career he played 279 matches taking 817 wickets (av. 23.52), scored 1,108 runs (av. 8.39) and held 103 catches. He represented England in 15 Tests between 1963/64 and 1972 taking 40 wickets (av. 23.52), scored 32 runs (av. 7.33) and held 7 catches. He toured overseas twice to India in 1963/64 and South Africa in 1964/65.

Norman Featherstone (1968–79). Born in Que Que, Rhodesia, in 1949, Norman Featherstone was a right-handed middle-order batsman and useful off-break bowler. He represented Middlesex between 1968 and 1979, playing 216 matches, and was capped in 1971. A member of the South African Schools Team to England in 1967, he made his first-class debut in South Africa for Transvaal 'B' in 1967/68 in the Currie Cup. He accumulated 8,882 runs (av. 28.65), bagged 137 wickets (av. 25.37) and held 185 catches for the county. His best performance with the bat was 147 versus Yorkshire at Scarborough in 1975, and with the ball 5 for 32 versus Nottinghamshire at Trent Bridge in 1978. His best season was in 1975 when he achieved 1,156 runs (av. 35.03) and against Kent at Canterbury he scored 127 not out and 100 not out. He received a benefit in 1979 and afterwards moved to Wales, where he represented Glamorgan from 1980 until the end of the 1982 season.

Mike Selvey (1972–82). Born in Chiswick, Middlesex, in 1948, Selvey was a right-arm fast-medium bowler and right-handed lower-order batsman. He represented Surrey in 6 matches between 1968 and 1971, before attaining a blue while at Cambridge University in 1971. He joined Middlesex in 1972 and played 213 matches for the county until 1982. He left Lord's after his benefit that year to take up the captaincy of Glamorgan between 1983 and 1984 when he was forced to retire after thirty-nine matches owing to injury. For the county he bagged 615 wickets (av. 25.45) with a best performance of 7 for 20 versus Gloucestershire in 1976. In the 1978 season he took 101 wickets (av. 19.09). He scored 1,835 runs (av. 12.48) with a top score of 67 versus Zimbabwe at Bulawayo in 1980/81 and held 56 catches. He played 3 Tests for England between 1976 and 1976/77 taking 6 wickets (av. 57.16), with a best performance of 4 for 41 versus the West Indies at Old Trafford in 1976, 15 runs (av. 7.50) and a single catch. He is now a well-known sporting journalist with the *Guardian* and broadcaster for BBC Radio's *Test Match Special*.

The 1973 team. Back row, left to right: D.A. Marriott, K.V. Jones, M.W.W. Selvey, P.H. Edmonds, N.G. Featherstone, T. Selwood, C.J.R. Black, H.A. Gomes. Front row: H.C. Latchman, M.J. Smith, F.J. Titmus, J.M. Brearley (captain), J.S.E. Price, J.T. Murray, C.T. Radley.

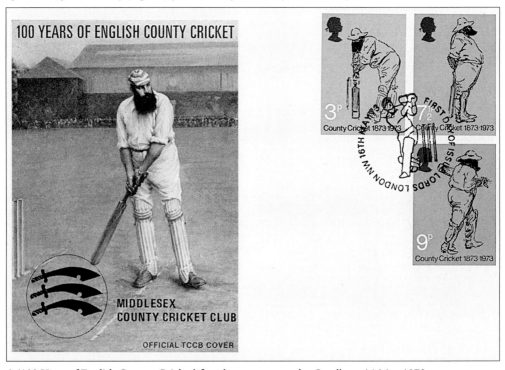

A '100 Years of English County Cricket' first day cover, posted at Lord's on 16 May 1973.

Benefit cricket at Lord's. Middlesex versus
Vic Lewis CC XI (F.J. Titmus' benefit).
Vic Lewis leads his team of all-stars through
the famous Lord's Pavilion Gates on to the
field of play in 1973.

Larry Gomes (1973–6). Born in Arima, Trinidad,
in 1953, Larry Gomes was a left-handed top-
order batsman, right-arm medium-pace or off-
break bowler and a good close fieldsman. He
represented his native Trinidad from 1971/72 to
1987/88 and Middlesex in 42 matches from 1973
to 1976. He scored 1,199 runs (av. 22.20) with a
top score of 93 not out versus Worcestershire at
Lord's in 1975; he collected 23 wickets (av. 40.13)
with a best of 4 for 22 versus Yorkshire at
Bradford in 1973 and held 11 catches. During his
career he amassed 12,982 runs (av. 40.56) with 32
centuries and a top score of 200 not out for the
West Indies versus Queensland at Brisbane in
1981/82. He represented the West Indies in
60 Tests between 1976 and 1986/87. He scored
3,171 runs (av. 39.64) with nine centuries
including a top score of 143 versus England at
Edgbaston in 1984, took 15 wickets (av. 62.00)
with a best of 2 for 20 versus Australia at Sydney
in 1981/82 and held 18 catches.

John Emburey (1973–95). An off-spin bowler and stubborn right-handed batsman, John Emburey was born in Peckham, London, in 1952. He played for Middlesex from 1973 in 376 matches taking 1,250 wickets (av. 24.09) with a best of 8 for 40 versus Hampshire at Lord's in 1993. He recorded 5 wickets in an innings fifty-eight times and 10 wickets in a match twelve times. He accumulated 9,053 runs (av. 24.40) with 7 centuries with a highest score of 133 versus Essex at Chelmsford in 1983, and held 368 catches. His best season was 1983 when he took 103 wickets (av. 17.33). He represented England in 63 Tests, twice as captain versus the West Indies in 1988. He took 147 wickets with a best of 7 for 78 versus Australia at Sydney in 1986/87 and scored 1,705 runs with a best performance of 75 versus New Zealand at Trent Bridge in 1986. He toured overseas on eight occasions although his international cricket appearances would probably have been greater had he not toured twice with unofficial rebel England teams to South Africa in 1981/82 and 1989/90. He played Currie Cup matches for Western Province between 1982 and 1984. In 1995 after his Testimonial season with Middlesex, he joined Northamptonshire for whom he played until 1997 before acting as County Coach until the end of the 1998 season.

The 1974 team. Back row, left to right: R.I.A. Nicholas (masseur), G.D. Barlow, J.E. Emburey, M.J. Vernon, P.H. Edmonds, M.W.W. Selvey, N.P.D. Ross, R.O. Butcher. Front row: K.V. Jones, C.T. Radley, M.J. Smith, J.M. Brearley (captain), F.J. Titmus, J.T. Murray, N.G. Featherstone.

The Hon. Tim Lamb (1974–7). Born in Hartford, Cheshire, in 1953, the younger son of Lord Rochester, Tim Lamb was schooled at Shrewsbury before going on to Oxford University. He made his first-class debut in 1973 and attained blues in both 1973 and 1974. He represented Middlesex in 36 matches between 1974 and 1977 before he moved to Northamptonshire for whom he played 108 matches between 1978 and 1983. For Middlesex he took 67 wickets (av. 30.31) with a best of 6 for 49 versus Surrey at Lord's in 1975; he scored 548 runs (av. 17.67) with a top score of 77 versus Nottinghamshire at Lord's in 1976 and held 13 catches. During his career with the ball, Lamb took 361 wickets (av. 28.97) with a best performance of 7 for 56 for Northamptonshire versus Cambridge University at Fenner's in 1980. With the bat he scored 1,274 runs (av. 12.49) and he also held 40 catches. He moved back to Lord's in 1983 when he was appointed Middlesex CCC Secretary/General Manager, a post he held until 1987, when he moved to the position of Cricket Secretary of the TCCB. In 1996, after the retirement of Alan C. Smith, he was appointed Chief Executive of the TCCB and subsequently the new England and Wales Cricket Board (ECB), which is now housed in new offices at the Nursery End of the ground at Lord's.

Roland Butcher (1974–90). Born in East Point, Barbados, in 1953, Roland Butcher was a right-handed middle-order batsman, right-arm medium bowler and an excellent fieldsman. He played his early cricket in Stevenage and represented Hertfordshire Schools prior to joining the Lord's groundstaff in 1969. He represented Middlesex from 1974 to 1990 and played 251 matches for the county scoring 10,935 runs (av. 31.69) with 17 centuries and a highest score of 197 versus Yorkshire at Lord's in 1982. He took 4 wickets (av. 40.25), with a best bowling performance of 2 for 37 versus Gloucestershire at Cheltenham College in 1986, and held 265 catches. Butcher represented Barbados in 1974/75 and Tasmania in 1982/83 and toured four times. He played 3 Tests and 3 one-day Internationals for England and was the first West Indian-born player to play Tests for England. His top score was 32 versus the West Indies at Kingston, Jamaica, in 1980/81. He was also a useful footballer and represented both Biggleswade Town and Stevenage Borough.

The 1975 team. Back row, left to right: Physiotherapist, M.W. Gatting, M.W.W. Selvey, P.H. Edmonds, M.J. Vernon, C. Whiteside, J.E. Emburey, T.M. Lamb, N.P.D. Ross, H.A. Gomes, G.D. Barlow, R.O. Butcher, I.J. Gould. Front row: J.S.E. Price, J.T. Murray, F.J. Titmus, J.M. Brearley (captain), M.J. Smith, C.T. Radley, N.G. Featherstone.

Phillipe Edmonds (1971–92). Born in Lusaka, Northern Rhodesia, in 1951, Phillipe 'Phil' Edmonds made his first-class debut for Middlesex in 1971 after taking 9 wickets versus Leicestershire at Fenner's in only his second first-class match for Cambridge University. He led Cambridge in his final year in 1973 before taking his slow left-arm skills to Lord's where he represented the county until 1987, although he did return for a single match in 1992. For Middlesex he played 257 matches, taking 883 wickets (av. 23.55) with a best performance of 8 for 53 versus Hampshire at Bournemouth in 1984. He recorded 5 wickets in an innings 39 times and 10 wickets in a match 8 times. He scored 5,036 runs (av. 19.82) with 2 centuries and a top score of 142 versus Glamorgan at Swansea in 1984. Edmonds played a total of 391 first-class matches, scoring 7,651 runs with a top score of 142 versus Glamorgan at Swansea in 1984. He took 1,246 wickets with a best of 8 for 53 versus Hampshire at Bournemouth in 1984 and held 345 catches. For England he played in 51 Tests between 1975 and 1987; touring overseas five times, he took 125 wickets with a best of 7 for 66 versus Pakistan at Karachi in 1977/78 and scored 875 runs. His wife, Frances, wrote accounts of his last two tours. Now engaged in business, he also writes and commentates on the game and is a member of the club's general committee.

Ian Gould (1975–96). Born in Taplow, Buckinghamshire, in 1957, Gould was a left-handed middle-order batsman and wicket-keeper. He represented Middlesex ninety-one times from 1975 to 1996 and was capped in 1977 before moving to Sussex which he represented 195 times between 1981 and 1990. For Middlesex he scored 2,109 runs (av. 20.88) with a single century, held 170 catches and took 26 stumpings. He also played one season in New Zealand for Auckland in 1979/80, captained Sussex in 1987 and played in 18 one-day Internationals for England. He played 297 first-class matches scoring 8,756 runs (av. 26.05) with four centuries and a top score of 128 for Middlesex versus Worcestershire at Worcester in 1978. He held 536 catches and took 67 stumpings and 7 wickets (av. 52.14) with a best of 3 for 10 for Sussex versus Surrey at the Oval in 1989. He toured abroad three times with Vic Lewis' XI to Pakistan in 1980/81, Middlesex to Zimbabwe in 1980/81, and with England to Australia and New Zealand in 1982/83. After retiring he returned to the county as 2nd XI coach.

Mike Gatting OBE (1975–98). Gatting, an aggressive right-handed batsman, right-arm bowler and fine fieldsman was born in Kingsbury, Middlesex, in 1957, and made his Middlesex debut in 1975 aged eighteen. He was capped at twenty. Appointed captain in 1983, he led the county until part-way through the 1996 season to three county championships. For Middlesex he played 412 matches, accumulating 28,411 runs (av. 52.80) with 77 centuries and 137 half-centuries with a top score of 258 versus Somerset at Bath in 1984. He took 129 wickets (av. 28.29) with a best performance of 5 for 34 versus Glamorgan at Swansea in 1982; he held 393 catches. His best season was 1984 when he accumulated 2,257 runs (av. 68.39). Representing England in 74 Tests, twenty-three as captain, he scored 4,227 runs with 9 centuries including a top score of 207 versus India at Madras in 1984/85. He toured overseas twelve times with various teams and his best tour was without doubt winning the Ashes and the Perth Challenge in Australia in 1986/87. He was awarded an OBE in 1987 for his services to cricket. He captained an unofficial rebel England tour to South Africa in 1989/90. Retiring from first-class cricket in 1998, his last match was against Derbyshire in the county championship. Since then he has been appointed the County Coach.

Benefit Cricket at Lord's – Middlesex versus Vic Lewis XI (M.J. Smith's benefit). Vic Lewis is seen batting at Lord's during the Mike Smith Benefit Match in 1975 with Bill Edrich, John Murray and Mike Brearley looking on; Mike Smith is the bowler. A collector of 6,000-plus cricket ties from all around the globe, Vic regularly designs ties for club beneficiaries and celebrations.

Middlesex county champions, 1976. Completed scorecard of the Surrey versus Middlesex championship match at the Oval when Middlesex won by 5 wickets and secured the county championship.

Middlesex team with the County Championship Trophy at Buckingham Palace in 1976. Left to right: Representative from Lord's Taverners, J.M. Brearley (captain), F.J. Titmus, P.H. Edmonds, M.J. Smith, G.D. Barlow, C.T. Radley, M.J. Vernon and N.D.P. Ross.

Middlesex committee members with the County Championship Trophy at Buckingham Palace in 1976. Left to right: M.P. Murray, R.V.C. Robins, R.A. Gale and M.O.C. Sturt.

Middlesex players share a few words at Buckingham Palace after receiving the County Championship Trophy in 1976. Left to right: Mike Selvey, Tim Lamb, Phil Edmonds (holding trophy) and Mike Smith.

MIDDLESEX COUNTY CRICKET CLUB

COUNTY CHAMPIONS 1976

Celebration Dinner

✧

23rd April, 1977

✧

In the Chair:

G. O. ALLEN ESQ. CBE

President

✧

Grosvenor House, Park Lane, London, W1

County Champions 1976 celebration dinner menu.

Players, officials and committee table at the 1976 County Champions celebration dinner.

Wayne Daniel (1977–88). Born in St Philip, Barbados, in 1956, the gentle, sensitive Wayne 'The Diamond' Daniel was without doubt an extremely quick right-arm fast bowler and right-handed tail-end batsman. He represented the West Indies in 10 Tests between 1975/76 and 1983/84 together with 18 one-day Internationals, and toured overseas on three occasions. He played for his native Barbados between 1975 and 1985 and joined Middlesex in 1977 after being noticed during the West Indies tour of England in 1976. He represented Middlesex 214 times taking 685 wickets (av. 22.02) recording 5 wickets in an innings 22 times and with a best performance of 9 for 61 versus Glamorgan at Swansea in 1982. His best season for the county was his benefit year in 1985 when he bagged 79 wickets (av. 26.72). As a tail-end batsman Daniel scored 1,043 runs (av. 10.32) with a top score of 53 not out versus Yorkshire at Lord's in 1981. He held 52 catches. A useful bowler in one-day domestic cricket, he took 7 for 12 against Minor Counties (East) at Ipswich and 6 for 17 against Sussex at Hove in the Benson & Hedges Cup in 1978.

Wilf Slack (1977–88). Born in Troumaca, St Vincent, West Indies, in 1954, Wilf Slack was a left-handed opening batsman and right-arm medium-pace bowler. His family emigrated from the Windward Islands to High Wycombe in Buckinghamshire when he was only eleven years old. He played his early cricket for Buckinghamshire in the minor county championship in 1976. He represented Middlesex in 210 matches between 1977 and 1988 and accumulated 12,565 runs (av. 40.53) including 25 centuries with a top score of 248 not out versus Worcestershire at Lord's in 1981. He took 19 wickets (av. 33.26) with a best performance of 3 for 17 versus Leicestershire at Uxbridge in 1982 and held 146 catches. Slack hit 1,000 runs in a season eight times with a best of 1,900 (av. 54.28) in 1985. He played 3 Tests for England between 1985/86 and 1986 scoring 81 runs (av. 13.50) with a top score of 52 versus the West Indies at St Johns, Antigua, in 1985/86 and held 3 catches. He toured overseas five times with Middlesex to Zimbabwe in 1980/81, Vic Lewis' XI to Pakistan in 1981/82, England 'B' to Sri Lanka in 1985/86, England to West Indies in 1985/86 and to Australia in 1986/87. He played for his native Windward Islands between 1981/82 and 1982/83. On three occasions while batting for Middlesex he collapsed but no reason could be found for these blackouts. He had been batting in an exhibition match in The Gambia in 1989 when he suddenly collapsed and died: a heart attack was found to be the cause. This was a sad loss for Middlesex cricket. A fitting tribute to his life is the 'Wilf Slack Memorial Cricket Ground', which is situated in Finchley, within a quarter of a mile of the Middlesex Indoor Cricket School and Sports Centre.

The 1977 Joint Championship winning team. Back row, left to right: D. Bennett (coach), I.J. Gould, M.W. Gatting, J.E. Emburey, N.P.D. Ross, T.M. Lamb, W.W. Daniel, W.N. Slack, R.P. Moulding, K.P. Tomlins, R.O. Butcher. Front row: G.D. Barlow, M.W.W. Selvey, C.T. Radley, J.M. Brearley (captain), M.J. Smith, N.G. Featherstone, A.A. Jones, P.H. Edmonds.

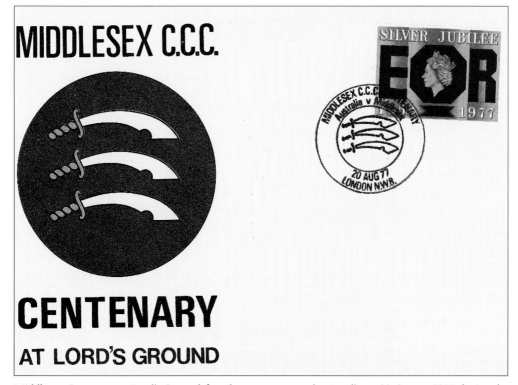

Middlesex Centenary at Lord's Ground first day cover – posted at Lord's on 20 August 1977 during the Middlesex versus Australia tour match.

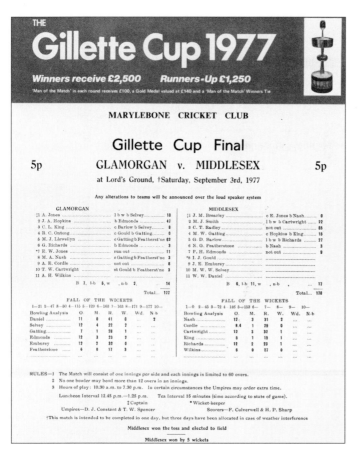

Completed scorecard of the Glamorgan versus Middlesex Gillette Cup Final in 1977.

Keith Tomlins (1977–85). Born in Kingston-upon-Thames, Surrey, in 1957, Tomlins was a right-handed middle-order batsman and right-arm medium-pace bowler. He represented Middlesex between 1977 and 1985 in 84 matches scoring 2,883 runs (av. 26.44) with 4 centuries, bagged 4 wickets (av. 81.50) with a best performance of 2 for 28, and held 63 catches. He moved to Gloucestershire for whom he played 24 matches between 1986 and 1987. During his career Tomlins accumulated 3,880 runs (av. 27.13) with five centuries, including a top score of 146 for Middlesex versus Oxford University at the Parks in 1982. He took just 4 wickets (av. 90.00) with a best of 2 for 28 for Middlesex versus Kent at Lord's in 1982 and held 66 catches. He toured overseas twice with Middlesex to Zimbabwe in 1980/81 and with Gloucestershire to Sri Lanka in 1986/87. In 1998 he was appointed the ECB cricket coach for the Western Region of England.

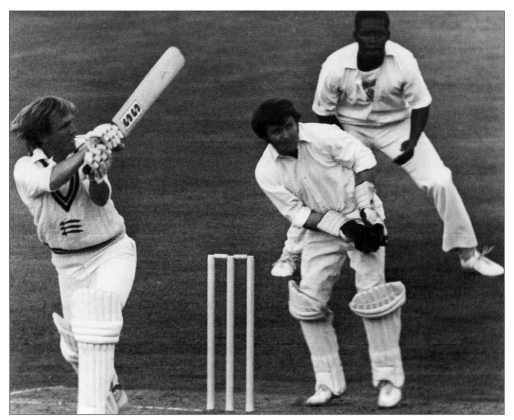

Clive Radley turns the ball to leg on his way to 85 in the Gillette Cup Final of 1977 against Glamorgan at Lord's. Wicket-keeper Efion Jones and slip Collis King look on.

Captain Mike Brearley holds the Gillette Cup trophy with Man of the Match Clive Radley in the 1977 Gillette Cup Final at Lord's.

Middlesex skipper Mike Brearley holds aloft the Gillette Cup with his team after having beaten Glamorgan at Lord's in 1977.

Gillette Cup Final official souvenir first day cover – posted at Lord's on 3 September 1977 when Middlesex beat Glamorgan by 7 wickets to win their first Gillette Cup.

Man of the Match Clive Radley, who scored an unbeaten 85 to guide Middlesex to victory, holds his medal and the Gillette Cup aloft on the Lord's Pavilion balcony in front of the large crowd.

1977 Joint Champions at Buckingham Palace, London. Left to right: K.P. Tomlins, H.P.H. Sharp (scorer), D. Bennett (coach), I.J. Gould, N.D.P. Ross, A.A. Jones, M.W.W. Selvey, the Duke of Edinburgh. From Kent: G.W. Johnson, N.J. Kemp, C.C. Lewis (scorer), D. Nichols, R.W. Hills, C.J.C. Rowe, G.S. Clinton and C.S. Cowdrey.

The 1978 team. Back row, left to right: W.N. Slack, W.W. Daniel, P.H. Edmonds, A.A. Jones, J.E. Emburey, N.G. Featherstone, G.D. Barlow, R.O. Butcher. Front row: M.W. Gatting, M.J. Smith, C.T. Radley, J.M. Brearley (captain), M.W.W. Selvey, I.J. Gould.

Graham Barlow (1969–86). Born in Folkestone in 1950, Barlow was a left-handed top-order batsman, right-arm medium bowler and superb outfielder. He joined Middlesex in 1969, was capped in 1976 and represented Middlesex 238 times until he retired after his benefit year in 1986. He amassed 11,640 runs (av. 35.48) with 23 centuries including a highest score of 177 versus Lancashire at Southport in 1981, took 3 wickets (av. 22.00) with a best of 1 for 6 and held 131 catches. He played 3 Tests for England with little success between 1976 and 1976/77 and toured overseas twice in 1976/77 to Australia, India and Sri Lanka. He also played 6 one-day Internationals for England. A sound opening batsman he was reliable in one-day domestic matches. He hit top scores of 158 versus Lancashire in the NatWest Trophy at Lord's in 1984, 129 versus Northamptonshire in the Benson & Hedges Cup at Northampton in 1977 and 114 versus Warwickshire in the John Player Sunday League at Lord's in 1979. Barlow suffered a hip injury in 1986 and visited a faith healer who advised him to strap a special stone to his leg at night to ease the problem. Having lived in South Africa since retiring, he became cricket coach at Haileybury School near Hertford in 1998.

Bill Merry (1979–82). Born in Newbury in 1955, Bill Merry was a right-arm medium-pace bowler and right-handed lower-order batsman. He represented Middlesex in 26 matches between 1979 and 1982 during which time the championship was won twice in 1980 and 1982, not to mention the last Gillette Cup against Surrey at Lord's also in 1980. He bagged 45 wickets (av. 32.15) with a best performance of 4 for 24 versus Somerset at Taunton in 1980; he scored 42 runs (av. 7.00) with a highest score of 14 not out versus Oxford University at the Parks in 1981 and held 6 catches. He toured overseas five times: with the MCC to Bangladesh in 1978/79, East Africa in 1981/82, Derrick Robins' XI to New Zealand in 1979/80 and Middlesex to Zimbabwe in 1980/81. He also played minor county championship cricket for Hertfordshire twice between 1976 and 1978 and 1983 and 1991. His last first-class match was for Minor Counties versus New Zealand at Lakenham, Norwich, in 1986.

The 1979 team. Back row, left to right: H.P.H. Sharp (scorer), D. Bennett (coach), I.J. Gould, M.W. Gatting, W.G. Merry, J.E. Emburey, R. Herkes, W.W. Daniel, N.J.H. Beardow, W.N. Slack, A.S. Patel, K.P. Tomlins, R.O. Butcher, J.E. Miller (physiotherapist). Front row: S.J. Poulter, A.A. Jones, P.H. Edmonds, M.J. Smith, C.T. Radley, J.M. Brearley (captain), M.W.W. Selvey, N.G. Featherstone, G.D. Barlow, C.F.E. Goldie.

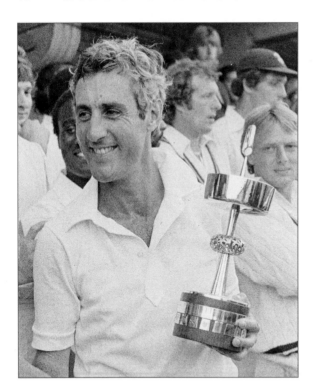

Mike Brearley, captain of Middlesex, watched by Paul Downton, with the Gillette Cup Trophy at Lord's Cricket Ground in 1980 after defeating Surrey by 7 wickets, having scored 96 not out.

Dressing room celebrations after the Gillette Cup Final victory over Surrey in the last of eighteen Gillette Cup Finals at Lord's against Surrey. Left to right: Clive Radley, Mike Smith, Vincent van der Bijl and skipper Mike Brearley.

Vincent van der Bijl (1980–1). Born in Rondebosch, Cape Town, South Africa, in 1948, the grandson of V.A. (Western Province), son of P.G.V. (South Africa) and great nephew of V.A.W. (Western Province), Vincent van der Bijl was a right-arm fast-medium bowler and right-handed lower-order batsman. Making his first-class debut for the South African Universities in 1967/68, he represented Natal between 1968/69 and 1981/82 and Transvaal in 1982/83 in the Currie Cup. He represented Middlesex in 1980/81 twenty-one times and helped the county to the double of the county championship and the Gillette Cup in 1980. For the county he bagged 86 wickets (av. 15.00) with a best performance of 6 for 47 versus Sussex at Hove in 1980; he scored 331 runs (av. 25.46) with a top score of 76 versus Nottinghamshire at Lord's in 1980 and held 5 catches. Van der Bijl topped the bowling averages for the 1980 season with 85 wickets (av. 14.72) and took 5 wickets in an innings on five occasions during the season, finishing with match figures of 10 for 69 versus Derbyshire at Uxbridge in 1980 when Middlesex won by 10 wickets. He was selected to tour twice with Wilfred Isaac's XI to England in 1969 and South Africa to Australia in 1971/72, but the latter tour was cancelled.

Middlesex celebrate winning the County Championship at Sophia Gardens, Cardiff, after beating home side Glamorgan. On the balcony of the Cardiff pavilion, left to right: Phil Edmonds, Graham Barlow, Vincent van der Bijl, Mike Brearley (captain), Harry Sharp (scorer), Mike Selvey, Simon Hughes, Wilf Slack and Keith Tomlins.

The 1980 Championship winning team. Back row, left to right: R.O. Butcher, P.R. Downton, W.G. Merry
W.W. Daniel, V.A.P. van der Bijl, M.W. Gatting, S.P. Hughes, H.P.H. Sharp (scorer). Front row: M.W.W. Selvey
C.T. Radley, J.M. Brearley (captain), P.H. Edmonds, G.D. Barlow, J.E. Emburey.

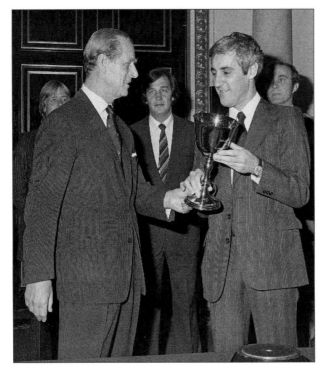

The Duke of Edinburgh presents the
County Championship Trophy to
Middlesex captain Mike Brearley at
Buckingham Palace in 1980. Bill
Merry, John Emburey and Phil
Edmonds look on.

The 1980 Champions at Buckingham Palace. Left to right: F.J. Titmus, M.J. Smith, R.O. Butcher, R.G.P. Ellis, the Duke of Edinburgh, W.G. Merry, J.M. Brearley (captain), J.E. Emburey, R.J. Maru, P.H. Edmonds, S.P. Hughes, P.R. Downton and M.W. Gatting.

Middlesex celebrate the County Championship with refreshments at Buckingham Palace in 1980. Left to right: R.J. Maru, R.G.P. Ellis, F.J. Titmus, R.O. Butcher, A.J. Burridge (Secretary) and E. Solomon (committee member).

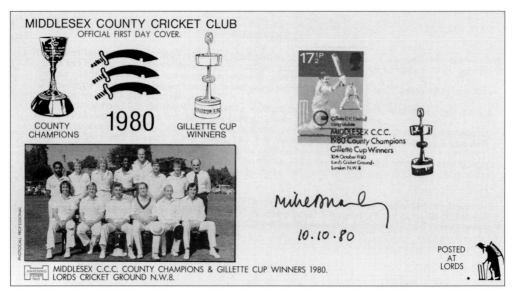

Middlesex Double Champions 1980 first day cover. It was posted at Lord's on 10 October 1980 to celebrate the double of the County Championship and the Gillette Cup, and signed and dated by Mike Brearley.

Testimonial lunch for long-serving Middlesex County Cricket Club Secretary Arthur Flower in 1980. Standing, left to right: Mike Brearley, Arthur Flower, Leslie Deakins, former Secretary of Warwickshire County Cricket Club, and John Warr – in the Banqueting Suite at Lord's Cricket Ground.

The 1981 team. Back row, left to right: D. Bennett (coach), R.J. Maru, R.O. Butcher, N.G. Cowans, J.R. Thomson, W.G. Merry, A.G. Smith, K.D. James, P.R. Downton, W.N. Slack, K.P. Tomlins, J.E. Miller (physiotherapist). Front row: J.E. Emburey, G.D. Barlow, C.T. Radley, J.M. Brearley (captain), P.H. Edmonds, M.W.W. Selvey, M.W. Gatting, W.W. Daniel.

Norman Cowans (1980–93). Born in Enfield St Mary, Jamaica, in 1961, Norman Cowans was on the Lord's groundstaff in 1979 and after a couple of years there he joined the Middlesex staff in 1980/81 for the tour of Zimbabwe. He made his county debut in 1981 and was a regular member of the team until 1993 when he left the county after his benefit year to join Hampshire. For Middlesex he played 188 matches. With his right-arm fast bowling he took 532 wickets (22.57) with 5 wickets in an innings eighteen times. His best bowling performance was 6 for 61 versus Leicestershire at Leicester in 1985. As a tail-end right-handed batsman his best score was 66 versus Surrey at Lord's in 1984. He played 19 Tests for England and toured overseas seven times. His best performances were both against Australia during 1982/83 when he took 6 for 77 at Melbourne and scored 36 at Perth. Cowans was capped in 1984 and was also a useful one-day bowler; in the Sunday League in 1991 against Lancashire at Lord's he returned figures of 6 for 9. Hampshire released him after two seasons in 1995.

Jeff Thomson (1981). Born in Sydney, Australia, in 1950, Jeff Thomson was a very fast right-arm bowler and right-handed late-order batsman. He was part of the most famous pace attack in Test cricket for much of the 1970s with partner Denis Lillee. Needing a replacement for the wonderful Vincent van der Bijl, who had proved a great success in 1980, the county turned to Jeff Thomson. 'Thommo', having represented New South Wales, Queensland and Australia in 34 Tests, arrived at Lord's on the back of Middlesex's 1980 double winning year. Early in the 1981 season the county took the field at Lord's for the first time with a team of eleven full international Test players. Playing only eight times for Middlesex in 1981 owing to injury, he took 23 wickets (av. 22.69), scored 63 runs (av. 12.60) and held 4 catches. His best performances of 4 for 66 and a top score of 35 came in the same match versus Essex at Lord's. His best performance during a disappointing season was 7 for 22 against Hampshire in the zonal group match of the Benson & Hedges Cup at Lord's.

Barbados Test Match, 1981. Seen here at Bridgetown, Barbados, are the Middlesex players included in the 1981 Test squad. Left to right: Mike Gatting, Paul Downton, Roland Butcher, Middlesex committee member Vic Lewis, Wayne Daniel (West Indies) and John Emburey.

Simon Hughes (1980–91). Born in Kingston-upon-Thames, Surrey, in 1959, Hughes was a right-arm fast-medium bowler and right-handed tail-end batsman. He represented Middlesex 172 times between 1980 and 1991, being capped in 1981. It was no surprise as a former Durham University student that he joined the new first-class county Durham immediately after his benefit year in 1991 in readiness for their inaugural season. For Middlesex he bagged 407 wickets (av. 30.11), scored 1,479 runs (av. 11.73) and held 42 catches. Hughes' best performances for Middlesex were 7 for 35 versus Surrey at the Oval in 1986 and 53 with the bat versus Cambridge University at Fenner's in 1988. He played for Durham until the end of the 1993 season, since when he has become a full-time sports journalist and television and radio commentator on cricket for the BBC.

Paul Downton (1980–91). Son of George, a Kent stumper of the 1940s, born a 'Man of Kent' in 1957, Downton was a wicket-keeper and useful right-handed batsman, who represented his native county from 1977 to 1979 as deputy to Alan Knott until his move to Middlesex in 1980. For Middlesex he played 219 matches scoring 6,891 runs (av. 29.07) with 6 centuries and a top score of 126 not out versus Oxford University at the Parks in 1986. He held 474 catches and took 63 stumpings and when asked to bowl took 1 wicket for 9 (av. 9.00) with a best of 1 for 4. He played 314 first-class matches during his career, scoring 8,270 runs and took 779 dismissals (690 catches, 89 stumpings). While scoring his maiden first-class century, 104, he also added 289 for the fifth wicket with Clive Radley versus Northamptonshire at Uxbridge in 1985. After suffering a freak eye injury when hit by a flying bail in the Sunday League match versus Hampshire at Basingstoke in 1990, he retired in 1991. For England he played 30 Tests, touring overseas seven times, scored 785 runs with a top score of 74 versus India at Delhi in 1984/85 and achieved 75 dismissals. Since retiring he has concentrated on working in the City and is a committee member of the club.

Neil Williams (1982–94). Born in Hope Well, St Vincent, West Indies, in 1962, Neil 'Nellie' Williams was a right-arm fast-medium bowler and a right-handed lower-order batsman. He represented Middlesex 193 times between 1982 and 1994 before moving after his benefit year to Essex in 1995. For Middlesex, he took 479 wickets (av. 30.63) with a best performance of 8 for 75 (12 for 139 in the match) versus Gloucestershire at Lord's in 1992. With the bat he accumulated 3,027 runs (av. 18.45), his highest score was 77 versus Warwickshire at Edgbaston in 1991, and he held 46 catches. He wintered playing for his native Windward Islands between 1982/83 and 1991/92 and Tasmania in 1983/84 in the Sheffield Shield. He represented England in a single Test at the Oval, scoring 38 runs and taking 2 for 148 against India in 1990 when Chris Lewis was forced to withdraw from the team owing to a migraine attack. Touring once with the English Counties to Zimbabwe in 1984/85, he played for Essex until the end of the 1998 season.

The 1982 Championship winning team. Back row, left to right: H.P.H. Sharp (scorer), D. Bennett (coach), C.R. Cook, W.N. Slack, N.J. Kemp, W.G. Merry, A. Smith, N.G. Cowans, K.J. James, N.F. Williams, P.R. Downton, R.O. Butcher, J.E. Miller (physiotherapist). Middle row: W.W. Daniel, G.D. Barlow, M.W.W. Selvey, M.W. Gatting, J.M. Brearley (captain), P.H. Edmonds, C.T. Radley, J.E. Emburey. Front row: G.M. Ritchie, R.J. Maru, S.P. Hughes, C.P. Metson, K.P. Tomlins.

The 1982 Champions at Buckingham Palace. Left to right: A. Wright (secretary), K.P. Tomlins, C.P. Metson, R.G.P. Ellis, J.M. Brearley (captain), J.D. Monteith, the Duke of Edinburgh, A.Smith, R.J. Maru, N.G. Cowans, M.W. Gatting, N.J. Kemp, A. Bennett and H.P.H. Sharp (scorer).

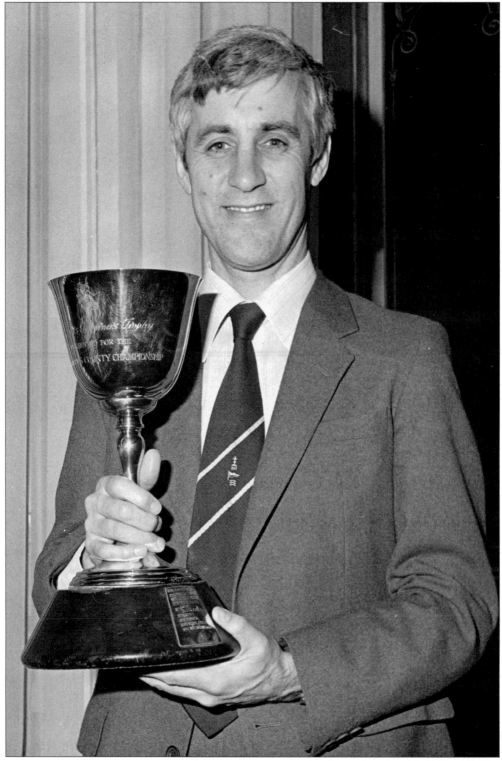

Middlesex captain Mike Brearley with the County Championship Trophy at Buckingham Palace in 1982.

CHAPTER EIGHT

GATTING AND BEYOND

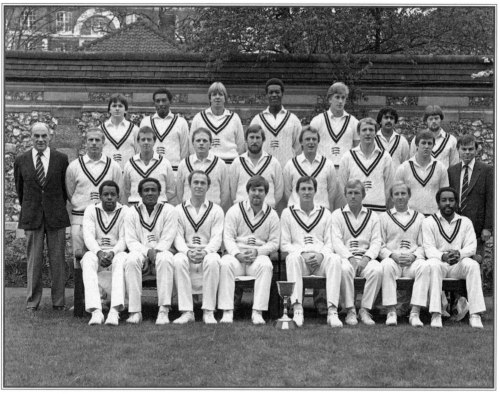

Middlesex 1983 team. Back row, left to right: C.P. Metson, N.F. Williams, W.G. Merry, N.G. Cowans, K.D. James, R.J. Maru, C.W.V. Robins. Middle row: H.P.H. Sharp (scorer), D. Bennett (coach), S.P. Hughes, K.P. Tomlins, C.R. Cook, P.R. Downton, A.G. Smith, K.R. Brown, J.E. Miller (physiotherapist). Front row: W.N. Slack, W.W. Daniel, P.H. Edmonds, M.W. Gatting (captain), J.E. Emburey, C.T. Radley, G.D. Barlow, R.O. Butcher.

John Carr (1983–94). Born in St John's Wood, London, in 1963, son of D.B. (Derbyshire and Oxford University), grandson of J.L. (Army), John Carr was a right-handed opening batsman, off-break bowler and useful fieldsman. Educated at Repton, he attained blues all three years between 1983 and 1985 while at Oxford University. He represented Middlesex in 191 matches between 1983 and 1996. He accumulated 9,846 runs (av. 39.54) with 20 centuries including a highest score of 261 not out versus Gloucestershire at Lord's in 1995, including 43 fours. He took 33 wickets (av. 35.03) with a best performance of 6 for 61 versus Gloucestershire at Lord's in 1985 and held 243 catches. He hit 1,000 runs in a season five times with his best season being 1994 when he achieved 1,543 runs (av. 90.76) including six centuries and seven fifties. He played minor county cricket for Hertfordshire in two spells between 1982 and 1984 and again between 1990 and 1991. In 1997 he was appointed the Cricket Operations Manager in the newly established ECB based at Lord's.

Clive Radley (Man of the Match) on his way to 89 not out, from a Middlesex total against Essex of 196 for 8 in 55 overs in the B&H Cup Final, 1983.

Clive Radley (Man of the Match) and Mike Gatting (captain) hold the Benson & Hedges Cup Trophy on the balcony at Lord's after Middlesex defeated Essex by the narrow margin of 4 runs.

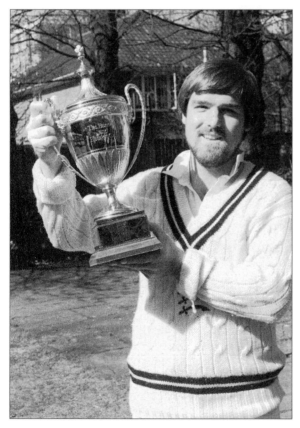

Mike Gatting holds the Benson & Hedges Cup, which was won in 1983 when they defeated Essex at Lord's.

The 1984 team. Back row, left to right: C.P. Metson, K.P. Tomlins, N.F. Williams, N.G. Cowans, K.R. Brown, S.P. Hughes. Middle row: J.E. Miller (physiotherapist), D. Bennett (coach), G.D. Rose, A.R.C. Fraser, J.F. Sykes, K.D. James, C.R. Cook, R.G.P. Ellis, H.P.H. Sharp (scorer). Front row: P.R. Downton, R.O. Butcher, J.E. Emburey, M.W. Gatting (captain), P.H. Edmonds, C.T. Radley, W.N. Slack.

Angus Fraser (1984–). Currently the finest right-arm medium-pace bowler available to England, Angus Fraser was born in Billinge, Lancashire, in 1965 and made his Middlesex debut in 1984. He was a permanent member of the county team until missing two complete seasons owing to back and hip injuries in 1991 and 1992. Making a welcome return the following summer, he assisted Middlesex to the County Championship, collecting 50 wickets. During the 1993 season he returned to the England team making his twelfth Test appearance versus Australia in the sixth Test at the Oval. He won the Man of the Match award by taking match figures of 8 for 131 to help England to their only victory of the Test series. For Middlesex he has played 185 matches, taken 554 wickets (av. 25.87) with a best performance of 7 for 40 versus Leicestershire at Lord's in 1993. He has recorded 5 wickets in an innings 19 times and 10 wickets in a match three times. He has scored 1,877 runs (av. 12.03) with a highest innings of 92 versus Surrey at the Oval in 1990 and has held 32 catches.

The dramatic last ball to give Middlesex victory over Kent at Lord's in the 1984 NatWest Trophy Final. John Emburey turns Richard Ellison for 4 to give Middlesex victory, having required one run to win off the last ball of the 60-over contest.

Middlesex's Clive Radley, having scored 67 runs, accepts the Man of the Match award and his NatWest Trophy Final tie after guiding Middlesex to victory in the 1984 Final against Kent at Lord's.

Mike Gatting accepts the NatWest Trophy after having defeated Kent in the Final at Lord's Cricket Ground by 4 wickets.

Mike Gatting and Clive Radley pose with the NatWest Trophy on the balcony at Lord's in 1984.

Mike Gatting holds aloft the NatWest Trophy
at Lord's after seeing off Kent.

Middlesex players pose with the NatWest Trophy Winners flag in 1984 at Lord's. Left to right:
S.P. Hughes, N.F. Williams, R.O. Butcher, P.R. Downton, W.N. Slack, M.W. Gatting (captain),
P.H. Edmonds, Lord Boardman (Chairman of NatWest Bank), J.E. Emburey, W.W. Daniel, N.G. Cowans,
C.T. Radley and G.D. Barlow.

The 1985 Championship winning team. Back row, left to right: P.C.R. Tufnell, K.R. Brown, N.R.C. MacLaurin, A.R. Harwood, G.K. Brown, S.P. Hughes, C.P. Metson. Middle row: J.E. Miller (physiotherapist), D. Bennett (coach), N.G. Cowans, J.F. Sykes, A.R.C. Fraser, G.D. Rose, W.N. Slack, N.F. Williams, K.P. Tomlins, H.P.H. Sharp (scorer). Front row: P.R. Downton, W.W. Daniel, G.D. Barlow, J.E. Emburey, M.W. Gatting (captain), C.T. Radley, P.H. Edmonds, R.O. Butcher.

Middlesex players celebrate winning the County Championship at Edgbaston after defeating Warwickshire by an innings and 74 runs in 1985.

Middlesex captain Mike Gatting pictured with the Britannic Assurance County Championship Trophy in 1985.

The Duke of Edinburgh shakes hands with Middlesex scorer Harry Sharp as Mike Roseberry, Keith Brown and Jamie Sykes look on.

Middlesex captain Mike Gatting introduces the Duke of Edinburgh to members of the Middlesex party. Left to right: George Mann, Mike Murray, Tim Lamb, Mike Sturt and Charles Robins.

The Duke of Edinburgh presents Mike Gatting of Middlesex with the 1985 County Championship Trophy at Buckingham Palace.

The 1985 Champions at Buckingham Palace. Left to right: P.C.R. Tufnell, C.T. Radley, N.G. Cowans, G.R. Brown, W.N. Slack, N.F. Williams, M.A. Roseberry, the Duke of Edinburgh, J.F. Sykes, P.R. Downton, M.W. Gatting (captain), K.R. Brown, J.E. Emburey, P.H. Edmonds, G.D. Rose, A. Harwood.

The 1986 team. Back row, left to right: A.R. Harwood, N.R.C. MacLaurin, K.R. Brown, J.D. Carr, M.A. Roseberry, P.C.R. Tufnell, A.J.T. Miller, C.P. Metson. Middle row: J.E. Miller (physiotherapist), A.G.J. Fraser, D. Bennett (coach), S.P. Hughes, J.F. Sykes, A.R.C. Fraser, G.D. Rose, N.G. Cowans, W.N. Slack, N.F. Williams, G.K. Brown, H.P.H. Sharp (scorer). Front row: R.O. Butcher, G.D. Barlow, C.T. Radley, J.E. Emburey, M.W. Gatting (captain), P.R. Downton, W.W. Daniel, P.H. Edmonds.

Top table celebrating Denis Compton's seventieth birthday in 1988. Left to right: John Warr, George Mann, Denis Compton and Keith Miller of Australia.

Phil Tufnell (1986–). Tufnell was born in Hadley
Wood, Hertfordshire, in 1966 and attended
schools in Highgate and Southgate before
making his Middlesex debut in 1986 versus
Lancashire at Old Trafford. A slow left-arm
spinner and right-handed tail-end batsman, he
soon established himself as an ideal replacement
'spin twin' for John Emburey after the
retirement of Phil Edmonds in 1987. For
Middlesex he has played 189 matches taking 639
wickets (av. 28.74) with a best of 8 for 29 versus
Glamorgan at Cardiff in 1993. He has recorded
5 wickets in an innings thirty times and 10
wickets in a match three times. He has scored
1,434 runs (av. 11.20) with a top score of 67
not out versus Worcestershire at Lord's in 1996
and has held 68 catches. He has represented
England in 20 Tests since making his debut
versus Australia at Brisbane in 1990/91 and has
now taken 60 wickets with a best of 7 for 47
versus New Zealand at Christchurch in
1992/93. He was awarded his county cap in
1990 and his best season came in 1991 when he
took 88 wickets. He is celebrating his benefit
season with the club in 1999.

The 1986 Benson & Hedges Cup Final team. Back row, left to right: R.O. Butcher, A.J.T. Miller,
W.W. Daniel, N.G. Cowans, W.N. Slack, S.P. Hughes, H.P.H. Sharp (scorer). Front row: P.R. Downton,
J.E. Emburey, M.W. Gatting (captain), C.T. Radley and P.H. Edmonds.

Mike Gatting, Middlesex skipper, holds aloft the Benson & Hedges Cup Trophy at Lord's in 1986 after Middlesex had defeated Kent by 2 runs.

The 1987 team. Back row, left to right: S.P. Hughes, A.J.T. Miller, K.R. Brown, G.K. Brown, J.D. Carr, M.A. Roseberry, A. Needham, M.R. Ramprakash. Middle row: D. Bennett (coach), A. Jones (2nd XI scorer), N.R.C. MacLaurin, P.C.R. Tufnell, J.F. Sykes, A.R.C. Fraser, A.J.G. Fraser, I.J.F. Hutchinson, N.F. Williams, N.G. Cowans, H.P.H. Sharp (scorer). Front row: W.N. Slack, P.R. Downton, C.T. Radley, M.W. Gatting, J.E. Emburey, W.W. Daniel, P.H. Edmonds, R.O. Butcher.

Mark Ramprakash acknowledges the Middlesex supporters, having reached his 50 in the NatWest Trophy Final versus Worcestershire at Lord's in 1988. He went on to score 56 valuable runs and win the Man of the Match award, with Middlesex gaining victory over Worcestershire by a margin of 3 wickets.

Mike Gatting accepts the NatWest Trophy from Lord Boardman, Chairman of NatWest Bank, at Lord's in 1988.

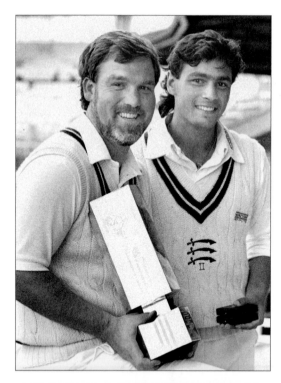

Mike Gatting and Mark Ramprakash pose with the NatWest Trophy on the balcony at Lord's in 1988.

Middlesex players pose with the NatWest Trophy Winners Flag in 1988 at Lord's. Left to right: R.O. Butcher, S.P. Hughes, J.E. Emburey, K.R. Brown, A. Habib, P.R. Downton, J.D. Carr, M.R. Ramprakash, P.N. Weekes, N.F. Williams, representative from NatWest, R.M. Ellcock, A.A. Barnett, M.W. Gatting (captain), I.D.F. Hutchinson, A.R.C. Fraser and N.G. Cowans.

The 1989 team. Back row, left to right: K.R. Brown, M.R. Ramprakash, R.M. Ellcock, I.J.F. Hutchinson, A.A. Barnett, P.N. Weekes, J.C. Pooley, A. Habib. Middle row: H.P.H. Sharp (scorer), D. Bennett (coach), M.A. Roseberry, P.C.R. Tufnell, A.R.C. Fraser, J.F. Sykes, A.G.J. Fraser, C.T. Radley, J.S.W. Davis (physiotherapist), A. Jones (2nd XI scorer). Front row: J.D. Carr, N.G. Cowans, P.R. Downton, J.E. Emburey, M.W. Gatting, R.O. Butcher, S.P. Hughes, N.F. Williams.

Desmond Haynes (1989–94). Born in Holder's Hill, Barbados, in 1956, 'Dessie' Haynes was an attractive right-handed opening batsman and right-arm medium and leg-break bowler. He represented his native Barbados between 1976/77 and 1991/92, acting as captain in 1990/91. He joined Middlesex in 1989, gained his cap in his first season and went on to represent Middlesex ninety-five times until 1994. He accumulated 7,071 runs (av. 49.10) including 21 centuries and with a highest score of 255 not out versus Sussex at Lord's in 1990. He also took 4 wickets (av. 48.00) with a best of 1 for 4 and held 48 catches. His best season was 1990 when he recorded 2,346 runs for the county. He also made over 4,000 runs in the three domestic limited overs competition with his highest score being 149 not out versus Lancashire at Old Trafford in the 1990 NatWest Trophy tie. He represented the West Indies in 111 Tests between 1977/78 and 1992/93, during which time he amassed 7,250 runs (av. 42.65) with 18 centuries and a top score of 184 versus England at Lord's in 1980. He toured nineteen times with the West Indies throughout the cricketing world. He represented Scotland in the Benson & Hedges Cup in 1983 and Western Province, South Africa, in the late 1990s. Since retiring he has concentrated on coaching serving Sussex, and is presently batting coach at Hampshire.

The 1990 Championship winning team. Back row, left to right: P. Farbrace, M.A. Roseberry, J.C. Pooley, P.N. Weekes, K.R. Brown, A.Habib. Middle row: H.P.H. Sharp (scorer), D. Bennett (coach), M. Keech, J.D. Carr, A.A. Barnett, J.R. Hemstock, I.J.F. Hutchinson, P.C.R. Tufnell, M.R. Ramprakash, J. Davis (physiotherapist), C.T. Radley (assistant coach), A. Jones (2nd XI scorer). Front row: S.P. Hughes, N.G. Cowans, P.R. Downton, J.E. Emburey, M.W. Gatting (captain), R.O. Butcher, N.F. Williams, D.L. Haynes. Inset: A.R.C. Fraser.

The 1990 Champions at Buckingham Palace. Left to right: C.T. Radley, P. Farbrace, H.P.H. Sharp (scorer), J.E. Emburey, the Duke of Edinburgh, A.R.C. Fraser, P.R. Downton, P.C.R. Tufnell, M.R. Ramprakash, M.A. Roseberry, N.F. Williams, S.P. Hughes, M.W. Gatting (captain), D.L. Haynes and D. Bennett (coach).

Middlesex captain Mike Gatting accepts the 1990 County Championship Trophy from the Duke of Edinburgh at Buckingham Palace.

Middlesex players and officials pictured outside Buckingham Palace in 1990 after receiving the County Championship Trophy from the Duke of Edinburgh.

Refuge Assurance Cup team, 1990. Back row, left to right: K.R. Brown, M.A. Roseberry, A.R.C. Fraser, P.C.R. Tufnell, M.R. Ramprakash, J.C. Pooley, P.N. Weekes. Front row: S.P. Hughes, N.G. Cowans, J.E. Emburey, M.W. Gatting (captain), D.L. Haynes, P.R. Downton.

Mike Gatting holds aloft the Refuge Assurance Cup at Edgbaston in 1990 after Middlesex had defeated Derbyshire by 7 wickets.

Double Champions again in 1990. Left to right: Bob Gale, Mike Gatting with the County Championship Trophy, John Emburey with the Refuge Assurance Cup and Phil Edmonds, at Lord's.

The 1991 team. Back row, left to right: R.J. Sims, T.A. Radford, R.M. Ellcock, J.C. Pooley, P.N. Weekes, M. Keech, A. Habib. Middle row: H.P.H. Sharp (scorer), D. Bennett (coach), P. Farbrace, C.W. Taylor, A.A. Barnett, M.R. Ramprakash, M.A. Roseberry, I.D.F. Hutchinson, D.W. Headley, S.M. Shepherd (physiotherapist), A. Jones (2nd XI scorer). Front row: N.F. Williams, P.C.R. Tufnell, N.G. Cowans, J.E. Emburey, M.W. Gatting (captain), P.R. Downton, K.R. Brown, A.R.C. Fraser.

The 1992 team. Back row, left to right: P. Farbrace, R.J. Sims, A. Habib, S.W. Sylvester, T.A. Radford, D.A. Walker, P.N. Weekes, M. Keech. Middle row: D. Bennett (coach), H.P.H. Sharp (scorer), I.J.F. Hutchinson, R.L. Johnson, J.C. Harrison, C.W. Taylor, R.M. Ellcock, J.C. Pooley, J.D. Carr, M.R. Ramprakash, D.W. Headley, A. Jones (2nd XI scorer), S.M. Shepherd (physiotherapist). Front row: P.C.R. Tufnell, K.R. Brown, N.F. Williams, J.E. Emburey, M.W. Gatting (captain), N.G. Cowans, A.R.C. Fraser, M.A. Roseberry, I.J. Gould.

County Team Six-a-Side Competition Winners at the Oval in 1992. Back row, left to right: D.L. Haynes, M.R. Ramprakash, J.D. Carr, A.R.C. Fraser, J.E. Emburey, M.A. Roseberry. Front row: M.W. Gatting (captain), K.R. Brown.

The Sunday League Trophy, which was won by Middlesex for the first time since 1969 after defeating Yorkshire at Uxbridge in 1992.

Celebration time at Park Road, Uxbridge, after Middlesex had seen off the visitors from Yorkshire to win their first Sunday League title. John Emburey, Mike Gatting and Angus Fraser share a joke or two.

The 1993 team. Back row, left to right: A. Habib, R.J. Sims, T.A. Radford, K.P. Dutch, P. Farbrace, M.A. Roseberry, M. Keech. Middle row: H.P.H. Sharp (scorer), S.M. Shepherd (physiotherapist), D. Bennett (coach), M.A. Feltham, J.C. Harrison, C.W. Taylor, R.L. Johnson, M.R. Ramprakash, P. Weekes, J. Pooley, I.J. Gould, A. Jones (2nd XI scorer). Front row: A.R.C. Fraser, P.C.R. Tufnell, N.F. Williams, J.D. Carr, M.W. Gatting (captain), J.E. Emburey, N.G. Cowans, K.R. Brown.

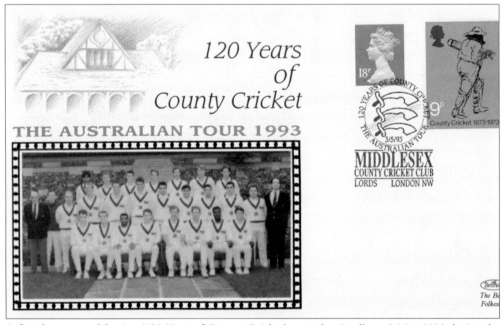

A first day cover celebrating '120 Years of County Cricket', posted at Lord's on 3 May 1993 during the Middlesex versus Australia tour match.

Albert Trott (1873–1914), a great cricketer for Australia, Middlesex and England. In early 1993 while reading *A Dictionary of Extraordinary English Cricketers* (Volume II) by J.L. Carr, the then Chairman of Middlesex CCC, Mike Murray, noticed that Albert Trott had committed suicide in 1914 and had since lain in an unmarked grave, plot P.613, in Willesden New Cemetery in north-west London. It was decided that a headstone should be placed on Trott's grave and on 22 May 1993 the anniversary of Trott's benefit match at Lord's in 1907 when he took four wickets in four balls followed by a hat-trick, the headstone was unveiled. The ceremony was attended by Revd Dr Melvyn Willshaw MA, BD, PhD, a member of the county, together with committee members Mike Sturt, Mike Murray, Charles Robins and Geoff Norris accompanied by Des Rundle and Bobby Simpson, the manager and coach respectively of the 1993 Australian Touring Team. Pictured here are Bobby Simpson, Revd Dr Melvyn Willshaw and Des Rundle.

Middlesex British Telecom phonecard, issued to celebrate their winning of the Britannic Assurance County Championship in 1993.

Middlesex County Cricket Club

CELEBRATION DINNER
1993 - WINNERS
Britannic Assurance County Championship
and
Rapid Cricketline 2nd XI County Championship
in
The Grand Ballroom
London Hilton on Park Lane   000437
on
Tuesday 19th April 1994

7.15 pm for 7.45 pm   **Dress: Lounge suit**

Ticket for Middlesex County Cricket Club celebration dinner in 1993.

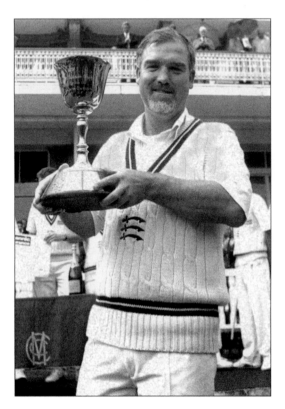

Mike Gatting holds aloft the County
Championship Trophy at Lord's in 1993.

Middlesex crowned Britannic Assurance County Champions at Lord's in 1993. Left to right: J.E. Emburey, D.L. Haynes, M.A. Roseberry, representative from Britannic Assurance, A.R.C. Fraser, M.W. Gatting (captain), N.F. Williams, P.C.R. Tufnell, M.R. Ramprakash, K.R. Brown.

The 1993 Championship winning team. Back row, left to right: S.M. Shepherd (physiotherapist), M.R. Ramprakash, P.N. Weekes, P.C.R. Tufnell, J.C. Pooley, M.A. Feltham, C.W. Taylor, M.A. Roseberry, R.L. Johnson, M. Keech, K.P. Dutch, R.J. Sims. Front row: N.G. Cowans, A.R.C. Fraser, N.F. Williams, J.D. Carr, M.W. Gatting (captain), J.E. Emburey, D.L. Haynes, K.R. Brown.

The Duke of Edinburgh in conversation with Middlesex players. From left to right: Mike Gatting (captain), Mark Ramprakash, Angus Fraser and John Carr at Buckingham Palace in 1993.

Mike Gatting receives the County Championship Trophy from the Duke of Edinburgh.

Denis Compton holds the County Championship Trophy in 1993 at Buckingham Palace. Left to right: Mike Murray, Alan Moss, Ivan Alter, Mike Sturt, Denis Compton, Mike Gatting (captain), Bob Gale, Joe Hardstaff (secretary).

Mike Gatting accepts the County Championship Trophy from the Duke of Edinburgh at Buckingham Palace in 1993 as Denis Compton looks on.

The 1993 Champions at Buckingham Palace. Left to right: M.A. Feltham, M.R. Ramprakash, M.A. Roseberry, R.J. Sims, K.P. Dutch, M.W. Gatting (captain), J.C. Pooley, A.R.C. Fraser, the Duke of Edinburgh, C.W. Taylor, J.D. Carr, R. Johnson, K.R. Brown, N.F. Williams, P.C.R. Tufnell, J.E. Emburey and representatives from Britannic Assurance and the Lord's Taverners.

The 1994 team. Back row, left to right: K.P. Dutch, P. Farbrace, P.N. Weekes, A. Habib, R.J. Sims. Middle row: S.M. Shepherd (physiotherapist), D. Bennett (coach), J.C. Pooley, M.A. Feltham, J.C. Harrison, C.W. Taylor, K. Marc, K.J. Shine, R.L. Johnson, I.J. Gould (2nd XI coach), A. Jones (2nd XI scorer). Front row: M.R. Ramprakash, A.R.C. Fraser, N.F. Williams, J.D. Carr, M.W. Gatting (captain), J.E. Emburey, M.A. Roseberry, K.R. Brown.

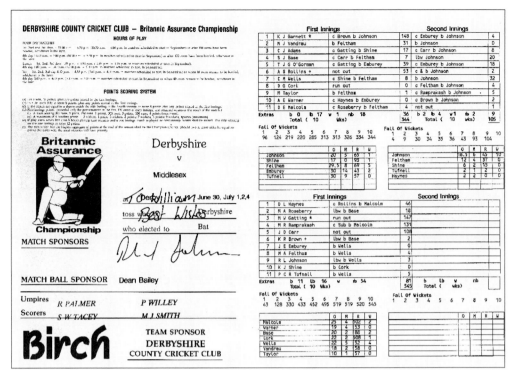

Scorecard for Derbyshire versus Middlesex Britannic Assurance Championship Match at Derby in 1994. Richard Johnson became the second youngest to take all 10 wickets in any first-class match when he took 10 for 45 versus Derbyshire at Derby in 1994.

The 1995 team. Back row, left to right: K.P. Dutch, A.A. Khan, D. Follett, J.C. Pooley, P.N. Weekes, T.A. Radford. Middle row: D. Bennett (coach), M.A. Feltham, R.L. Johnson, D.J. Nash, C.W. Taylor, K. Marc, K.J. Shine, J.C. Harrison, P. Farbrace, A. Jones (2nd XI scorer), I.J. Gould (assistant coach). Front row: M.R. Ramprakash, J.E. Emburey, M.W. Gatting (captain), J.D. Carr, A.R.C. Fraser, K.R. Brown.

The 1996 team. Back row, left to right: D. Follett, S.P. Moffat, P.E. Wellings, K.P. Dutch, O.A. Shah, A.A. Khan, D.C. Nash. Middle row: S.M. Shepherd (physiotherapist), D. Bennett (coach), R.L. Johnson, I.N. Blanchett, M.R. Evans, R.A. Fay, J.C. Harrison, D.J. Goodchild, J.P. Hewitt, U.B.A. Rashid, M.A. Feltham, A. Jones (2nd XI scorer), I.J. Gould (assistant coach). Front row: P.C.R. Tufnell, M.R. Ramprakash, J.D. Carr, M.W. Gatting (captain), A.R.C. Fraser, K.R. Brown, P.N. Weekes, J.C. Pooley.

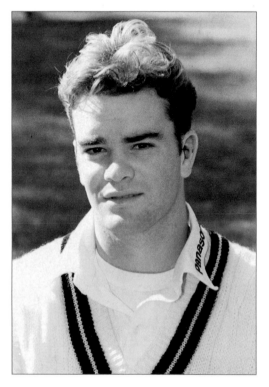

Dion Nash (1995–6). Born in Auckland, New Zealand, in 1971, Dion Nash is a right-arm fast-medium bowler and a lower order right-handed batsman. After an impressive performance for New Zealand versus England at Lord's in the second Cornhill Test of the 1994 series, when he scored 56 runs and took 6 for 76 and 5 for 93 (match figures of 11 for 169), the county signed him and he made his debut for Middlesex in 1995 and was capped in his first season. He promised much but suffered injury in his second season and despite trying hard to regain his fitness his contract was terminated at the end of the 1996 season. For Middlesex he played 21 matches scoring 448 runs (av. 19.47), bagged 53 wickets (av. 29.35) and held 11 catches. His best performances were 67 with the bat versus Essex at Chelmsford and 5 for 35 with the ball versus Hampshire at Lord's, both in 1995. He represented Northern Districts twice between 1990/91 and 1991/92 and again since 1995/96, Otago from 1992/93 to 1993/94. He has played 17 Tests for New Zealand between 1992/93 and 1998.

The 1997 team. Back row, left to right: K.P. Dutch, S.P. Moffat, P.E. Wellings, M.R. Evans, A.W. Laraman, A.J. Strauss, N.D. Martin. Middle row: S.M. Shepherd (physiotherapist), D. Bennett (coach), D.C. Nash, D.F. Lye, J.M. de la Pena, J.P. Hewitt, R.A. Fay, J.C. Harrison, I.N. Blanchett, D.J. Goodchild, U.B.A. Rashid, O.A. Shah, I.J. Gould (assistant coach), A. Jones (2nd XI scorer). Front row: J.C. Pooley, P.C.R. Tufnell, A.R.C. Fraser, M.W. Gatting, M.R. Ramprakash (captain), K.R. Brown, R.L. Johnson, P.N. Weekes.

Jacques Kallis (1997). Born in Pinelands, Cape Town, in 1975, Jacques Kallis is a right-handed top-order batsman, useful right-arm fast-medium bowler and an excellent slip fieldsman. He has represented his native Western Province since 1993/94 and made his debut for Middlesex in 1997 playing 16 matches. He was capped in his initial season with the county. He accumulated 1,034 runs (av. 47.00) with 4 centuries including a highest score of 172 not out versus Worcestershire at Kidderminster. He took 32 wickets (av. 20.46) with a best performance of 5 for 54 versus Kent at Lord's and held 15 catches. He won the Man of the Match award in the NatWest Trophy second round game when he scored exactly 100 and took 4 for 47 versus Gloucestershire at Uxbridge. Kallis has represented South Africa in 19 Tests since 1996/97 scoring 842 runs (av. 29.03) with two centuries, of which his highest score was 132 versus England at Old Trafford in 1998. He is one of the younger generation of talented batsmen presently playing Test cricket.

Justin Langer (1998). Born in Perth, Western Australia, in 1970, Justin Langer is a left-handed top-order batsman, right-arm medium bowler and occasional wicket-keeper. He has represented his native Western Australia in the Sheffield Shield since making his debut in 1991/92 and has played more than a dozen Tests for Australia. He has toured six times with Australia, to England in 1995 and 1997, South Africa in 1996/97, West Indies in 1994/95 and New Zealand in 1992/93 and 1994/95. His highest career score was 274 not out for Western Australia versus South Australia at the WACA, Perth, in 1996/97. Langer was capped in 1998 and enjoyed a good initial season with the county playing 15 matches. While scoring 166 against Essex, he added a county record of 372 for the first wicket with Mike Gatting (241) at Southgate in 1998 and completed the season with 1,448 runs (av. 62.95) with 4 centuries, of which his highest was 233 not out versus Somerset at Lord's. He took a single wicket against Northamptonshire at Lord's and held 12 catches.

The 1998 team. Back row, left to right: A.J. Strauss, R.A. Kettleborough, J. Langer, S. Cook, I.N. Blanchett, U.B.A. Rashid, D.C. Nash. Middle row: I.J. Gould, S.M. Shepherd (physiotherapist), O.A. Shah, B. Hutton, T. Bloomfield, J. Hewitt, A.W. Laraman, D.J. Goodchild, K.P. Dutch, N.D. Martin, J. Buchanan (coach), J. Maunders, A. Jones (2nd XI scorer). Front row: R.L. Johnson, J.C. Pooley, P.C.R. Tufnell, K.R. Brown, M.R. Ramprakash (captain), M.W. Gatting, A.R.C. Fraser, P.N. Weekes.

Richard Johnson (1992–). Born in Chertsey, Surrey, in 1974, Richard Johnson is a right-arm fast bowler and left-handed late-order batsman. He made his county debut in 1992 and was capped in 1996. In 1994 he became the second youngest to take all ten wickets in any first-class match when he bagged 10 for 45 versus Derbyshire. He toured India with England 'A' in 1994/95 and he was selected for England's winter tour to South Africa in 1995/96 but he had to decline due to injury. With the ball, he has taken 207 wickets (av. 27.42) with a best of 10 for 45 at Derby in 1994; he has recorded 5 wickets in an innings on five occasions and 10 wickets in a match twice. With the bat he has scored 1,183 runs (av. 14.08) with a highest innings of 50 not out versus Cambridge University at Fenner's in 1994. He has held 26 catches. In the 1997 season he took 47 championship wickets (av. 27.17) and in 1998 he took 50 (av. 27.38).

Mark Ramprakash (1987–). Born in Bushey, Hertfordshire, in 1969, Mark Ramprakash made his debut for the county in 1987 and was capped in 1990. A right-handed top-order batsman, right-arm medium bowler and excellent close fieldsman he has captained the county since half-way through the 1997 season when Mike Gatting handed him the job. Playing 186 matches for the county he has accumulated 13,029 runs (av. 49.91) with 40 centuries and 61 half-centuries. His highest score is 235 versus Yorkshire at Headingley in 1995. He has taken 18 wickets (av. 51.05) with a best of 3 for 32 (5 for 65 in the match) versus Glamorgan at Lord's in 1998 and held 95 catches. Ramprakash has represented England in 29 Tests scoring 1,195 runs (av. 24.89) with a top score of 154 versus the West Indies at Bridgetown, Barbados, in 1998, has taken 3 wickets (av. 102.66) with a best of 1 for 2 and held 20 catches. He has also played in thirteen one-day Internationals scoring 265 runs (av. 26.50) with a top score of 51. He has scored one day domestic centuries in all competitions for Middlesex: 104 versus Surrey at Uxbridge in 1990 in the NatWest Trophy, 119 not out versus Northamptonshire at Lord's in 1994 in the Benson & Hedges Cup and 147 not out versus Worcestershire at Lord's in the Sunday League in 1990.

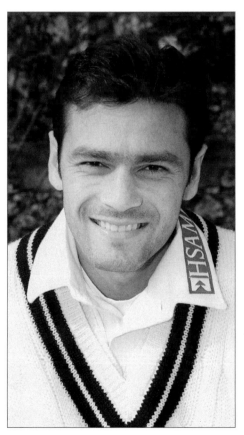

Owais Shah (1996–). Born in Karachi, Pakistan, in 1978, Owais Shah is a right-handed middle-order batsman, off-break bowler and useful fieldsman. He made his county debut in 1997 and has played 31 matches for the county. He has scored 1,546 runs (av. 36.80) with 3 centuries including a top score of 140 versus Yorkshire at Lord's in 1998. He has taken 2 wickets (av. 61.00) with a best of 1 for 24, and has held 26 catches. He captained England U19 in the World Cup in South Africa in 1997/98 and against Pakistan during the 1998 domestic season. He is a promising youngster for the future, both for club and country.

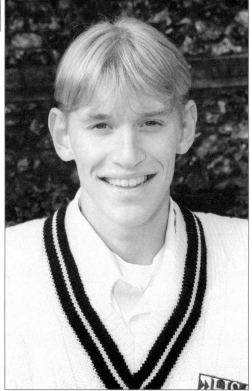

Jamie Hewitt (1996–). Born in Southwark, London, in 1974, Jamie Hewitt is a right-arm fast bowler and right-handed late-order batsman. He made his county debut in 1996, and has played 43 matches for Middlesex since taking the wicket of Gloucestershire's Richard Dawson with his first ball in first-class cricket. With the ball, Hewitt has taken 125 wickets (av. 27.58) with a best of 6 for 14 versus Glamorgan at Cardiff in 1997, and has recorded 5 wickets in an innings on four occasions. With the bat he has scored 844 runs (av. 18.75) with 3 fifties and a highest innings of 75 versus Essex at Chelmsford in 1997, and held 16 catches. In the 1997 season he took 57 championship wickets (av. 23.70) showing he has a promising future with the county.

CHAPTER NINE

LORD'S & OTHER MIDDLESEX GROUNDS

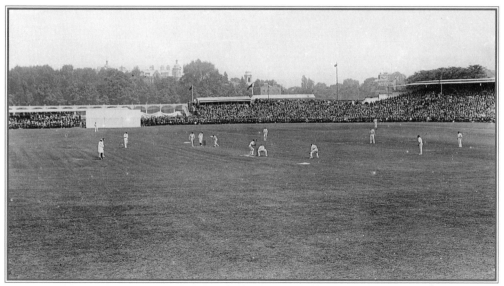

*A view of Lord's Cricket Ground, looking from the Pavilion towards the Nursery End and with the old
Mound Stand, to the right of the picture, 1905.*

*Apart from Lord's Cricket Ground in St John's Wood, Middlesex have played first-class matches at a
number of other venues in central London and the county of Middlesex. On 22 September 1736 a match
between Middlesex and Surrey was played at Lamb's Conduit Fields, now Coram Fields. This area has
now been built upon by the Brunswick Shopping Centre near Great Ormond Street Hospital. Other
matches followed at such venues as Hampton Court Green near Hampton Court Palace in 1762, the
Honourable Artillery Company Ground off Chiswell Street in the City between 1763 and 1771 and
Stamford Hill in 1768. A year later in 1769 a match was staged at Stanmore Common and on 31 May
1787 Middlesex played their first match at the first Lord's Ground, where Dorset Square is now situated,
near Marylebone station.*

The Pavilion at Lord's Cricket Ground in 1917.

The Grace Gates were erected in 1923 at the main members' entrance to the ground in St John's Wood Road, next to the famous Lord's Tavern Public House and Banqueting Suite.

OTHER GROUNDS

In 1790 Middlesex staged a match against the MCC at Uxbridge Moor. This area now houses the Uxbridge Industrial and Trading Estate to the south of Cowley Millet Lane. After a brief period at North Bank, Thomas Lord settled on the present third Lord's Ground in St John's Wood Road and since 1814 matches have been played on this ground. In 1877 the MCC agreed that Middlesex could play all their home matches at Lord's from that time. The county has taken some matches away from Lord's since 1877, and these included visits to the Walker Cricket Ground at Southgate in 1859, 1991 and 1998. The Cattle Market Ground in Islington was used between 1864 and 1868 for 15 matches and Lillie Bridge in West Brompton near Chelsea's Stamford Bridge was used in 1871 when Surrey were the visitors. Between 1873 and 1876 Middlesex played 13 championship matches at Prince's Ground in Knightsbridge and a single match between 23 and 25 June 1887 at Chiswick Park. The visitors were Oxford University who won the match by an innings and 229 runs thanks to K.J. Key's 281 not out, of a total of 555.

In 1959 the county staged a championship match away from Lord's at Tivoli Road, the home of Hornsey CC in north London, within sight of Alexandra Palace. Middlesex suffered defeat at the hands of Hampshire by 2 wickets thanks to a fine 155 from Jimmy Gray for the visitors. In 1980 cricket was taken to Park Road (subsequently named Gatting Way), Uxbridge, the home of Uxbridge CC, and matches have been played there regularly since. In 1981 a tour match was staged at Watford Town CC's Woodside ground in Garston when Sri Lanka beat Middlesex by 2 runs despite 58 from Keith Tomlins. A year later in 1982 Enfield CC's Lincoln Road ground staged a NatWest Trophy first round match with Cheshire who were disposed of by 8 wickets thanks to 5 for 12 from Phil Edmonds and 54 not out from Wilf Slack. Finally matches were staged at Laleham Burway near Chertsey, Kennington Oval in 1870 and 1939 and Essex's ground at Chelmsford in 1977 when Lord's was unavailable.

A view of the Lord's Tavern as it was in 1948 before demolition and the construction of the New Tavern Stand.

An aerial view of Lord's Cricket Ground in 1948.

A match in progress in 1953 with the old Tavern and Mound Stands in the background.

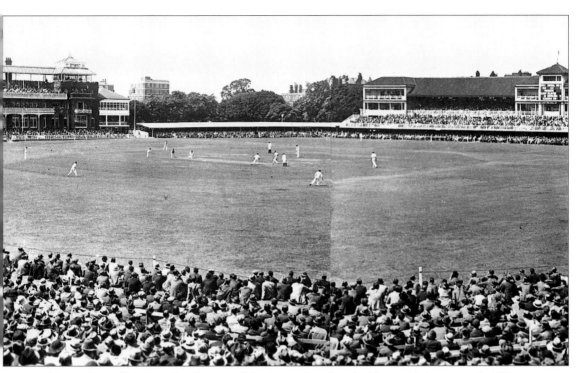

A view of the Pavilion, old 'A' Stand enclosure and the former Grandstand with a match in progress in 1953.

The Pavilion at Lord's Cricket Ground, 1955.

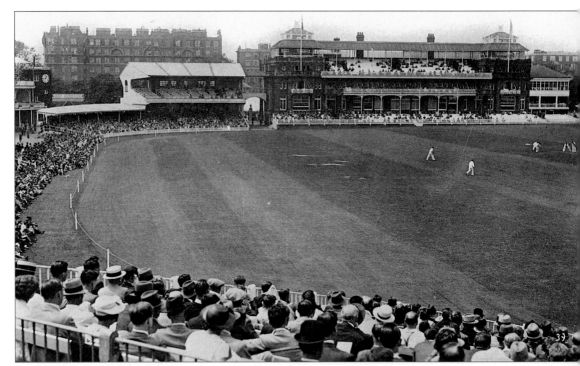

The Pavilion, the 'Q' Stand (latterly renamed the Sir George Allen Stand) and the old Tavern Stand as it looked in 1954

The excavations from the railway tunnels below the Wellington Road end of the ground at Lord's provided banking fo the original Mound Stand, which was built in 1898/99 on the area that was previously the old tennis and racket courts This picture and those opposite illustrate the Mound Stand in 1920, 1981 and 1991.

The Mound Stand, 1981.

The Mound Stand, 1991.

The Pavilion, Sir George Allen Stand and the Warner Stand viewed from the Nursery End of the Lord's Cricke
Ground during the Axa Equity & Law Sunday League match between Middlesex and Kent, 1993.

Middlesex versus Hampshire at Tivoli Road, Hornsey, in 1959. Alexandra Palace can be seen in the background.

Action from the NatWest Trophy first round tie at Lincoln Road, Enfield, when Middlesex took on minor county side Cheshire, July 1982. Phil Edmonds has bowled David Bailey round his legs as wicket-keeper Paul Downton and close fieldsman Mike Brearley, Clive Radley and umpire Nigel Plews look on.

Established in 1789, Uxbridge Cricket Club claims to be the oldest club in Middlesex, although its ground at Park Road was only inaugurated in 1971. Middlesex were first approached to play a match at Uxbridge in 1979 but this Prudential World Cup warm-up match was cancelled because of poor weather. Seen here is a view of the pavilion during the close season.

Vincent van der Bijl bowling at Uxbridge during the match when he bagged 10 for 89 and set up Middlesex for their 10-wicket victory over opponents Derbyshire in 1980.

Middlesex played their initial first-class match at Uxbridge, defeating Derbyshire by 10 wickets. Seen here is a view of the ground taken during that match.

Well-known faces in the Uxbridge crowd. Left to right: Arthur Flower, Vic Lewis, 'Tadge' Webster, Gubby Allen and Eddie Solomon watch play during the County Championship match with Derbyshire at Uxbridge in 1980.

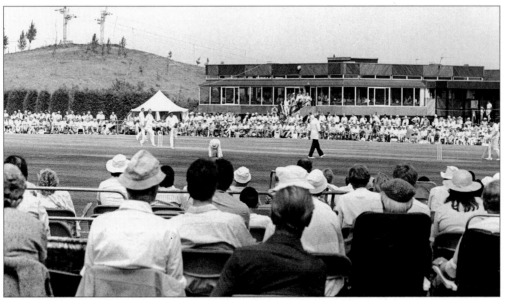

The ground at Uxbridge is part of a large sports complex providing facilities for squash, football, tennis and bowls as well as a swimming pool and a dry ski slope. The pavilion has been extended since it was constructed during the winter of 1970/71 and this now includes squash courts and additional members' bar, which is used as a players' dining area during Middlesex county matches. The former Middlesex and England spin bowler Phil Edmonds opened the County Bar and viewing area in 1981. This picture shows a view of the county match staged in 1993.

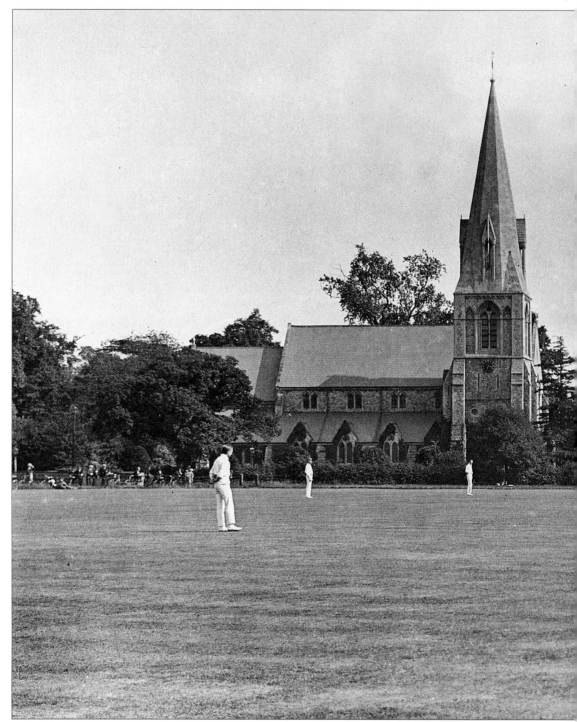

The Walker Cricket Ground has been the home of the Southgate Cricket Club since its foundation in 1855. The most famous Middlesex cricketing family, the seven Walker brothers, all played their early cricket at the ground now situated in Waterfall Road, Southgate; the ground was given the name 'The Walker Cricket Ground' by a deed of trust in December 1907. Mr Russell Walker, the last surviving brother, signed the document. The record attendance for the

nly first-class match at Southgate was around 10,000 for the game between Middlesex and Kent in 1859. Middlesex played only their second first-class match at the ground in 1998 when Essex were the second visitors to the Waterfall Road Ground. Seen here is a view of the Walker Cricket Ground looking towards Christ Church in Waterfall Road during the Southgate versus the MCC match on 18 June 1910.

Having played at Southgate back in 1859, it was not until 1991 that Middlesex returned to the Walker Cricket Ground to stage a Sunday League match versus Kent. Angus Fraser is bowling during the 1991 match and the game is being played beneath the nearby Christ Church.